VOLTAIRE

STUDIES IN LANGUAGE

AND LITERATURE

CONSULTING EDITOR:

HASKELL M. BLOCK

BROOKLYN COLLEGE OF

THE CITY UNIVERSITY OF NEW YORK

VOLTAIRE

A CRITICAL STUDY

OF HIS MAJOR WORKS

BY

1314

VIRGIL W. TOPAZIO

RICE UNIVERSITY

RANDOM HOUSE

NEW YORK

to

NORMAN L. TORREY,

the incomparable progenitor of Voltairean scholars,

with affection and admiration

CONTENTS

VOLTAIRE

CHAPTER I

THE MAN

AND HIS BACKGROUND

*T*hroughout a long lifetime, Voltaire devoted himself religiously, as inappropriate as that word may seem, and with a dedication unmatched in his day or since, to the unwelcome task of eradicating the weeds of wickedness, misery, and injustice in the human garden. And because new weeds continuously grow in a soil made fertile by human selfishness and greed, the message of Voltaire needs repetition, just as the moral exhortations of spiritual leaders must perforce be repeated to parishioners, too prone from one Sunday to the next to forget the pitfalls of unchecked passions. So skillfully did he employ each literary genre to propagate his ideas, that he was the indisputable master of all of them in his own time and is still considered unsurpassed in some of them.

It has become commonplace to view Voltaire as the great champion of human rights, the incomparable foe of injustice and social abuses, whose potent weapon of ridicule made the mighty, even kings, tremble before its satiric thrusts. For posterity he continues to be the outstanding advocate of reason and common sense, the relentless antagonist of any action or thought that is unable to withstand the searching scrutiny of reason. Hence metaphysics, religious dogma, and the selfish or tyrannical use of power in any field of human endeavor automatically became tarof his wrath. He was, in the best sense of the term, the apostle of reason employed for the betterment of mankind. To this day he epitomizes all that the *philosophes* of the eighteenth century stood for in their battle to free man from the shackles imposed by religion and government. Sacrilegious as it may at first sound, "Humanity may never find its salvation until Voltaire is canonized." [1]

To understand Voltaire one must recognize that he was the outstanding representative of classicism during the Age of Enlightenment. Whatever innovations he may have incorporated in his works, especially in his theater, he remained true to the classical ideal of the physiological oneness of man rooted in reason and nature. The ironist in Voltaire would have made him appreciate the twist of fate that caused him to survive as the prose stylist of his century, for no man utilized or defended poetry more knowingly than he. "Until the publication of the *Siècle de Louis XIV* (*Age of Louis XIV*) in 1751," Gustave Lanson tells us, "Voltaire was incontestably associated with poetry in the minds of his contemporaries; his glory was there." [2] Indeed, Voltaire's most marked seventeenth-century prejudice was his preference for poetry over prose, a prejudice he retained to his dying day.

In some ways Voltaire remained more classical than the seventeenth-century neo-classicists. The changes he introduced may have marked him as an innovator, but he was firmly entrenched in the past. His insistence upon anchoring religious principles in man instead of in faith—which after all could and did vary from people to people—was in conformity with the best classical outlook. And the Natural Law upon which Voltaire founded his theories of justice—subject of the main struggles of his life—was likewise "the logical deduction from the classical persuasion of the oneness of humanity." [3] Most of the changes he incorporated in his tragedies were essentially a reaction against what he felt were restrictions upon the freedom of the dramatist; they did not signify his opposition to the classical ideal. Few writers, and certainly none in the eighteenth century, surpassed Voltaire in literary taste, which is the distinguishing mark of most classical writings. It was this attribute that endeared him over a span of more than fifty years to the

Marquise du Deffand, the veteran defender of classicism. A century and a half later, the great Voltairean, Gustave Lanson, could convincingly argue that Voltaire displayed a sense of taste even in his most scurrilous and pornographic works.

A distinction should be made between the seventeenth- and eighteenth-century concepts of reason, for though Voltaire's century was called the Age of Reason, the writers and philosophers of the preceding age had also sung its praises, following the lead of Descartes. In the seventeenth century, reason was primarily philosophic rationalism, the rationalism of a St. Thomas Aquinas or a Descartes, which relied upon the reasoning processes following the *a priori* acceptance of traditional postulates. The Cartesian and Pascalian use of reason had followed a surrender, however partial, to the emotions, quite different from the surrender witnessed in Jean-Jacques Rousseau's more radical revolt. In the eighteenth century, on the other hand, the appeal to reason was definitive; there were no escapes at hand from the verdicts rendered by experience and experiment. And as the role of the sciences increased, the shift in emphasis was from the rational to the experimental in the application of reason. In this respect, Voltaire lagged behind such staunch supporters of experimental philosophy as Diderot and d'Alembert. We find him clinging tenaciously to the rational principle of Natural Law in matters such as religion and ethics, whereas in the sciences he wholeheartedly adopted the experimental approach as early as the Cirey period.

Voltaire spent the first twenty years of his life during the reign of Louis XIV, yet he lived to become the symbol and embodiment of eighteenth-century enlightenment and progress. The son of a notary, he evinced at an early age a penchant for literature and found a sympathetic milieu in the distinguished clients of his father, Francois Arouet, and especially among the literary friends of his mother, Marguerite Daumard, a member of the lesser nobility, who died when he was seven years old. His godfather, the Abbé de Châteauneuf, a notable representative of classical culture and libertarian thought of the day, early fostered and directed his talented godson's literary taste, so that by time he entered the famous Jesuit Collège Louis-le-Grand, the path he was later to follow was already well defined. At school he not only received the typical seventeenth-century education, which was firmly entrenched in classical tradition, but had the unusual opportunity of cultivating the friendship of members of many of the most important families of the time, friendships that were to stand him in good stead throughout his life. Some, such as d'Argental (the nephew of his enemies Mme. de Tencin and her brother the Cardinal de Tencin), Cideville, and the two d'Argenson brothers (sons of the First Lieutenant of Police), remained his lifetime friends.

The education Voltaire received at Louis-le-Grand from the Jesuit fathers Thoulié, Lejay, Tournemine, Tarteron, and Porée encouraged rather than discouraged the talents of their precocious protégé for wit and poetry. Their interest in dramatics likewise set afire young Arouet's passion for the theater, a dominant characteristic of his long literary career. The seven years he spent under the guidance of the Jesuits confirmed his literary aspirations, kindled an equally strong desire to succeed socially, and gave shape to his rebellious spirit. One of Voltaire's actions at Louis-le-Grand accurately prefigured his destiny. To circumvent a school rule that permitted no heat before ice had begun to form in the holy water, Voltaire, whose physical frailty caused him to suffer unduly from the cold, slyly placed some ice in the basin. His behavior throughout his life followed a similar pattern—he was always inclined to subserve reasons to Reason, especially in matters where human welfare was at stake.

To the consternation of his bourgeois-minded father, the social contacts that the latter had hoped would benefit his son in establishing a sound career had instead enticed the son beyond the reach of paternal control and certainly destroyed whatever willingness there may have been to pursue the monotonous and stodgy life of a notary. The gay life of the Temple, the licentiousness of the Regency period, and the influence of Abbé Chaulieu reinforced the natural bent of this witty adolescent toward a somewhat tempered epicureanism or rational hedonism, in which the *bonum* of life was to live happily. "In the company of these distinguished nobles and most unchurchly churchmen (the freethinkers of the *Société du Temple*), the young man," according to George Havens, "sharpened his gift for repartee and ironic wit, developed his natural tendency toward religious skepticism, practiced the graceful art of badinage and light society verse, and formed his literary taste." [4] In addition to the libertine appreciation of life, the Abbé Chaulieu had instilled in his young disciple a belief in the nonsectarian God of deism and a love of classicism. These became the foundation stones upon which Voltaire built a philosophy and an enduring code of ethics. In the meantime the courtier in him flourished. His mischievous and often bawdy verse served as his *entrée* to the salons of the mighty of his day. Wit being the most prized of coins, Voltaire cultivated his natural talents and quickly acquired a reputation that on several occasions was to bring down misfortune on his head. The irresistible life of pleasure and the unrestrained license of the Regency held so much appeal for the young Voltaire, that the emergence of the mature, socially-oriented thinker was a slow process. To some extent he never entirely succeeded in discarding the mantle of the dilettante and courtier (his enemies would substitute for these terms "parasite" and "sycophant").

An overweening vanity kept alive his insatiable need to outwit his companions in the intellectual duels at salons and other social gatherings. Lulled into a false sense of security by the ease with which his exceptional talents gained for him the companionship of nobility, Voltaire frequently cast caution to the winds. Too easily forgotten were the harsh realities of eighteenth-century social stratification, which made it impossible for a bourgeois, however right or gifted, to deal on equal terms with noblemen. In all probability he often forgot that he was *bourgeois*. In those days, when exile was a common punishment for having incurred the displeasure of the court, a separation from Paris was normally sufficient. Sometimes the simple abstention from participation in court functions was all that was required, depending upon the severity of the king's displeasure. Voltaire suffered many such banishments, as well as two imprisonments. The first incarceration in the Bastille for eleven months (1717–1718) was for his "J'ai vu" against the Regent, Philippe d'Orléans, which was presumably written by a minor poet, Le Brun. Such was Voltaire's reputation, however, that no one doubted its authorship. He spent the time in prison writing verses for his epic poem, *La Henriade,* and quite probably polishing *Oedipe* (*Oedipus*), his first tragedy, for the future presentation of which he had painstakingly cultivated all his contacts at the Comédie Française. The imprisonment apparently left no visible scars; he emerged the same insouciant and ambitious young man, with only one goal—success in society and literature. The astounding success of the more than forty successive presentations of *Oedipe* in 1718 was not designed to steady an easily turned head. Instead, intoxicated by his fame, he changed his name from Arouet to de Voltaire. All seemed normal again, and it is difficult to know whether one should blame the times or Voltaire's insulation from the realities of existing social conditions.

The second stay in the Bastille in 1726 resulted from his having dared to challenge the Chevalier de Rohan-Chabot, the nobleman who had repaid Voltaire's audacious repartee with a caning. "The blows administered by the Rohan canes," Emmanuel Berl has remarked, "definitely put an end to that period of youthful folly." [5] After two weeks in the Bastille he was released on condition that he leave the country. For the first time, the social inequality in France impressed Voltaire, who had been previously protected by his influential associations and his own clever mind. This blow to his human dignity sharply reminded him of the insignificance of the bourgeoisie in the eyes of the privileged ruling classes. The two and a half years spent in England only served to reinforce this realization of injustice and intolerance in France. Works written before his sojourn in England had of course already revealed the Voltairean stamp: *Oedipe* (1718) and "Epître à Uranie" ("Epistle to Uranie," 1722); even *La Henriade* (1723) was as forthright an indictment of the Saint-Bartholomew massacre as a panegyric of Henry IV.

the exact truth may be about the formative in-
English period upon Voltaire, it is clear that
ng poet of thirty-one was not yet the writer
day or the intrepid champion of justice.

His various experiences in England unquestionably left an imprint on his mind. Newton's funeral in 1727 drove home the difference between England and France in the respect paid to arts and letters. Striking too was the English climate of tolerance and justice, which stood in contrast to his first-hand knowledge of France. Happily for Voltaire, while he was in that marvelous country in which young noblemen did not shrink from delving into commerce, he developed a financial astuteness, thanks probably in part to his stay with Sir Everard Falkener. One immediate result was the successful publication of *La Henriade* in England through popular subscription. The more lasting effects were the successes he enjoyed in his subsequent speculations, which made him very rich and independent.

After his return to France, the rebellious instinct really emerged, and the courtier yielded to the humanitarian in such works as the *Histoire de Charles XII* (*History of Charles XII*, 1732). The process of change was hastened by the occurrence of new sparks that fired his indignation. One such was the treatment of Adrienne Lecouvreur, one of the most beautiful and talented actresses of the day. Voltaire was still at the stage in which personal involvement was necessary to set him afire. Adrienne had not only been his mistress but had, with Thieriot, nursed him through a serious attack of smallpox in 1723. To see her denied burial in consecrated ground by persons who had shortly before applauded her artistry was more than the volatile Voltaire could bear. Throwing caution to the winds, he consented to the dissemination of his "Ode sur la Mort de Mademoiselle Lecouvreur" ("Ode on the Death of Mlle. Lecouvreur," 1730) and in a letter to Thieriot wrote: "were the troupe of the devout, always inflamed with pure zeal, to surround my body with faggots, and all for the good of my soul, I cannot help releasing these verses, which were dictated by indignation, tenderness, and pity" [Best. 394].[6]

Some of this wrath, although moderated by the passage of time and transmuted by the requirements of the literary genre, manifested itself in the *Lettres philosophiques* (*Philosophical Letters*), which Voltaire had already started to write. He could no longer content himself with sporadic thrusts at chinks in the religious and political armor, meanwhile regaling himself within the "enemy camp" and depending upon his ability to please to insure his comforts and safety. The condemnation of the *Lettres philosophiques* in 1734 and the order for his arrest completely destroyed Voltaire's equanimity and whatever pleasure he had derived from pitting his wit and skills against existing conditions. Fortunately Voltaire had recently made the acquaintance of Mme. du Châtelet, the former mistress of Voltaire's friend, the Duc de Richelieu, a woman who was as interested in intellectual matters as she was in sensual ones. He went to live with her at Cirey, where (from all available accounts) the two "philosophers" worked harder than they played. Voltaire's correspondence contained many complaints about the lack of sufficient peace and solitude to work effectively, for with the passing years hard work had become for him a necessity and a consolation. Cirey provided the ideal place for a happy combination of work and pleasure. They were sixteen fruitful years. Especially significant is the interest in the sciences that Emilie du Châtelet instilled in Voltaire. Many were the hours they spent in their well-equipped laboratory, built, as were the other additions to Cirey, at Voltaire's expense. And though the initial interest may have been expressed to please Emilie, he applied himself with enough seriousness to produce several scientific works, the most important of which are: "Eléments de la philosophie de Newton" ("Elements of Newton's Philosophy," 1738); "Memoire sur la nature du feu" ("Memoir on the Nature of Fire," 1738); "Dissertation sur les forces motrices" ("Dissertation on Motor Forces," 1741)—the last two submitted to the Academy of Sciences; and "Dissertation sur les changements arrivés dans notre globe et sur les pétrifications qu'on prétend en être les témoignages" ("Dissertation on the Changes that Have Occurred on Our Planet and on the Petrifications that Are Claimed to Be Proof Thereof," 1744).

In spite of Emilie and the laboratory, Voltaire remained at best a knowledgeable amateur. Neither his interest in nor his grasp of the sciences equaled Diderot's, as evidenced by his inclination to reserve reason and common sense as the final court of appeal where scientific decisions were involved. And in some sciences, such as biology and geology, he never managed to keep abreast of the progress being made. As late as 1741, the seventeenth-century classicist in Voltaire was still denouncing the tendency of the sciences to dominate and crush poetry. Nonetheless, the prolonged experience did manage to moderate Voltaire's limited and unjust evaluation of the role of the pure sciences. Heretofore he had insisted upon the utility or practicality of any study: "There is a point beyond which research becomes a matter of mere curiosity; their ingenious and useless truths resemble the stars which, far from us, do not give us any light" [XXII: 186].[7] To some extent this remained his conviction, for it must be said that his too great reliance on common sense and reason produced a literal-minded outlook.

From a literary point of view, the Cirey years were very productive: the most important plays are *Alzire, Mahomet,* and *Mérope;* he also wrote "Le Mondain" ("The Worldly Man"), *La Pucelle (The Maid)*, and other numerous poetic works. Posterity has judged to be more significant, however, the historical works he undertook in order to prove to Emilie that history could and should be more than just a succession of dates and a recitation of royal deeds. The *Siècle de Louis XIV* and the monumental *Essai sur les moeurs et l'esprit des nations (Essay on the Manners and Spirit of Nations)*, were written in large part during this period. And important from a literary point of view was the fact that Voltaire seriously adopted the *conte* as an effective vehicle for his philosophic ideas. *Le Monde comme il va, vision de Babouc (Babouc, or the World as It Is)*, *Memnon, Scarmentado,* and the more famous *Zadig* were written at this time, primarily to entertain his aristocratic friends. He wrote *Zadig* at Sceaux, the château of the Duchesse du Maine, the wife of the bastard son of Louis XIV and Mme de Montespan. Voltaire at first thought these tales to be trifles unworthy of publication; their enthusiastic reception soon convinced him of their true potential.

Early during Voltaire's stay at Cirey a noteworthy event took place. The twenty-four-year-old Crown Prince Frederick of Prussia started corresponding with Voltaire, on August 8, 1736. Frederick, who fancied himself a poet, admired Voltaire as the greatest poet and historian of the age and therefore earnestly sought his friendship and guidance. The first letter read in part: "Your poems merit the study of honest men. They are a school of morals in which one learns to think and act" [Best. 1081]. In the second letter he followed the lead subtly suggested by Voltaire and delighted the heart of the poet-philosopher with these words: "Regard my actions henceforth as the fruit of your teachings. . . . Cirey will be my Delphi, and your letters, which I beg you to keep writing me, my oracles" [Best. 1139]. Future developments made it clear that Frederick was more interested in having his poetry corrected by the outstanding poet of Europe and his language polished by the most eminent practitioner of French. For Voltaire the correspondence offered an unparalleled opportunity to render mankind a service by inculcating in this future monarch a respect for tolerance and the dignity of man. Voltaire is still accused by some of having been motivated by selfish reasons, but the plain truth is that he always placed humanity above self. Even his ventures into diplomacy, notably in 1742 and later during the Seven Years War, although they leave some doubt as to his diplomatic ability and even his patriotism, were motivated by a sincere desire to prevent war, the world's greatest evil.

Like most geniuses, Voltaire was not cut from a single bolt of cloth. The increasing seriousness with which he viewed religious and political intolerance had not yet succeeded in submerging the lighter side so well illustrated by his poem "Le Mondain." Newton, he observed, would have been a much more delightful person had he also written some comedies. The mid-forties saw Voltaire achieve his greatest successes at Court after the death of Cardinal de Fleury in 1743. Many factors contributed to the favorable climate that affected Voltaire's change of fortune. D'Argenson, his friend of long standing, became War Minister in 1743 and Minister of Foreign Affairs the following year. Another friend, Mme. d'Etioles, better known as Mme. de Pompadour, had acquired enormous power and influence as the mistress of the king and served to counteract the dislike of two other powerful enemies, Boyer, Bishop of Mirepoix, and Maurepas, Fleury's successor. Ironically, even Voltaire's diplomatic missions to Prussia in

1742 and 1743 as an emissary, first of Prime Minister Cardinal de Fleury and then of Richelieu and Amelot, for all that they were failures, had added to his prestige and increased his stature at Court. Favors and honors descended upon Voltaire. In 1745 he was named historiographer of King Louis XV, and he set out to add greater meaning and luster to the position, although the historiographer could descend to the role of courtier in "Poème sur la victoire de Fontenoy" ("Poem on the Victory of Fontenoy") in 1745. Such sycophantic chores brought further royal approbation in the form of an appointment as *gentilhomme ordinaire du roi*. And the same year, thanks to his ingenuity (his detractors would say "deceit"), he cleverly played upon the Pope's vanity in order to secure his approval of *Mahomet*, intrinsically an anti-religious play. With his worst enemy, Bishop of Mirepoix, rendered harmless, Voltaire's election to the French Academy quickly followed, an honor richly deserved and long overdue. Voltaire fully recognized his role during this period for what it was. In a letter to the Abbé Duvernet, his future biographer, he expressed deep regret at having wasted these years so shamelessly.

It is interesting to speculate, in view of Voltaire's own conviction that inconsequential incidents often play key roles in the determination of great actions, as to what kind of life he might have lived had certain episodes not come to mar what seemed on the surface to be an established career and existence at Court. The exchange in English between Emilie and Voltaire at the *jeu de la reine*, which placed in doubt the honesty of others at the gaming table, was unfortunately understood. The two found it expedient to leave hastily under cover of darkness. They fled to the chateau of Sceaux, where he began to write philosophical tales. While there, they accepted an invitation to visit Lunéville, the minuscule capital of Lorraine. Stanislas, the former king of Poland and father of Marie Leczinska, the queen of France, ruled over this tiny kingdom. His confessor, who despised Mme. de Boufflers, the king's mistress, had invited Mme. du Châtelet in the hope that she would replace Mme. de Boufflers in the king's favor. Emilie's sensual nature, long denied by Voltaire's increasing physical incapacities, did find an outlet—not with the king, but with a handsome young captain who happened to be a visitor at Lunéville, the virile Saint-Lambert. The consequences of this ill-fated liaison were Emilie's pregnancy and her subsequent death in childbirth. Voltaire suddenly found himself bereft of his loved one, the woman who had been his companion for sixteen years. Even though their relationship had become more and more platonic, the emotional wrench was evident in his letters and behavior during the period immediately following her death. Their friendship, strengthened rather than lessened by the diminution in physical intimacy, had been sufficiently profound to survive his having caught Saint-Lambert and Emile *in flagrante delicto,* and to undertake the delicate task of convincing M. du Châtelet, that he, Châtelet, was the father.

For years Emilie had prevented Voltaire from accepting the insistent invitations of Frederick, who had become king of Prussia in 1740. To be sure, Voltaire was at the time involved in an intimate relationship with his widowed niece, Mme. Denis, a liaison that had started while he was still living with Emilie. Despite the letters to his niece, many of them in Italian, which might erroneously paint Voltaire as a man of insatiable sensual appetites, the relationship between uncle and niece did not enslave Voltaire. The best of his passion was spent vicariously in letters or bawdy poems; he was never a great Don Juan. In short, after Emilie's death Voltaire was really free for the first time to accept Frederick's invitation. Moreover, conditions at Court facilitated his decision: he had fallen into disfavor and Louis XV openly favored his rival Crébillon. How could he any longer resist the entreaties of a king who sang his praises and wooed him in verse?

The ever-scheming Frederick, realizing that the time was propitious to add Voltaire to his retinue, played his trump card. He appealed to Voltaire's ego by seeing to it that he learned that his former protégé, Baculard d'Arnaud, was about to supplant the master. The stratagem succeeded. Pride and vanity overcame the last reservation: the desire to extract enough money from Frederick to defray the traveling expenses to Potsdam for his niece, with whom he was living at that time. The long-delayed trip was made in 1750, and this action was to change the course of his life.

Whatever truth there may be to La Mettrie's charge that Frederick was interested only in having the supreme master of the French language by his side long enough to perfect his French and correct his poetry before discarding him like a squeezed orange, it was clear from the start that these two prima donnas were not destined to live long together without an eruption. Two incidents shattered any possibility for a peaceful existence at the Court of so capricious a despot. First there was Voltaire's failure to curb his instinctive desire to make a financial profit whenever the opportunity presented itself. Where money was concerned, Voltaire displayed "a curious admixture of splendid generosity with virulent tenacity. . . . He could haggle endlessly over 14 cords of firewood with the President de Brosses from whom he had leased Tournay and without a second thought decline to accept the thousand louis offered by the Duchess of Saxe-Gotha for the *Annales de l'Empire*." [8] When confronted with the chance to buy stocks that promised great profits—a financial speculation expressly forbidden by the king—Voltaire simply could not resist, even though as Chamberlain of the king his actions increased the likelihood of embarrassing Frederick. He attempted to circumvent the royal edict by acting through an intermediary by the name of Abraham Hirschel. Later, furious at the realization that he had been victimized, he threw all caution to the winds and instituted legal action against Hirschel. The questionable financial manipulations of the court Chamberlain thus became public knowledge, much to Frederick's disgust.

The second incident annoyed Frederick even more, since Voltaire's ridicule of Maupertuis, the respected President of the newly-formed Prussian Academy, reflected upon the court itself. No longer having a restraining hand to check his natural impulse to outshine everyone about him, Voltaire had antagonized Maupertuis and made him resentful of Voltaire's unchallenged brilliance and superiority at court functions. When Koenig clashed with Maupertuis over the latter's explanation of nature by the law of least effort, the former minimized the importance of the idea, asserting that Leibnitz had already entertained the same idea and discarded it. Maupertuis, by the force of his authority and probably with the tacit approval of the king, had Koenig condemned as a forger. A study of Koenig's defense convinced Voltaire of his innocence. Enraged by the injustice and heedless of the obvious risk of further alienating the king, he leaped into the fray with the only weapons he possessed: his wit, ridicule, and literary skills. The result was the *Diatribe du Docteur Akakia* (*Doctor Akakia's Diatribe*), which Frederick ordered burned publicly by the executioner. The break had become inevitable, and Voltaire was ordered to leave. His departure was not to be accomplished, however, without that final confrontation with royal power and caprice that was demonstrated in the traumatic incident at the Frankfort border, where he and Mme. Denis, who had joined him, were detained for days until the poetry demanded by the king arrived from Leipzig.

The two and a half years spent in Germany had not been wasted, in spite of the tendency of some critics to allow Voltaire's somewhat frenetic life to obscure the fact that he was always a conscientious writer, seriously dedicated to his art. No matter where he found himself, the days were invariably spent alone and hard at work, and Potsdam was no exception. A list of his major publications during that three-year period is eloquent testimony: *Siècle de Louis XIV* (1751), *Micromégas* (1752), *Défense de Milord Bolingbroke* (1752), "Poème sur la Loi Naturelle" ("Poem on Natural Law," 1752), in all likelihood a version of *Sermon des cinquante* (*Sermon of the Fifty*), and in addition several plays and many articles for the *Dictionnaire philosophique* (*Philosophical Dictionary*).

A grave dilemma confronted Voltaire after his expulsion from Germany. Where should he establish himself? It was evident that Louis XV would not be pleased to see him return to Paris. Germany was out of the question after that last indignity suffered at the hands of Frederick II. Geneva presented a problem of its own. Being a Catholic and therefore unable to own property in Geneva, he had to buy Les Délices under Dr. Theodore Tronchin's name. Two years later he also purchased a home in Lausanne, yet the two homes on Swiss soil did not erase his feeling of insecurity. Since the Calvinists disapproved of his theatrical activities, he was convinced he needed additional protection. He found this in the two properties of Tournay and Ferney (acquired three years later), which were on French soil, yet sufficiently close to the border to permit quick transfer from one property to another as prudence and safety dictated. Within a few years the homeless Voltaire had become the wealthy landlord of four considerable estates. The "cultivation-of-his-garden" phase of life, so vaunted in *Candide* as a way of life, had begun. At first it was more of a pastime at Les Délices, but increasingly he became more and more earnest. After installing himself permanently at Ferney, he was devoting all the capital and energies that were not expended in writing on the development of industries and the establishment of a full-fledged colony of workers. Factories that produced watches and silk stockings flourished under his guidance. He became the beloved and benevolent patriarch of an entire community, the Voltaire immortalized by Houdon, the person most usually visualized today when the name of Voltaire is mentioned. Once installed at Ferney, where he remained until his final return to Paris and death in 1778, Voltaire knew freedom for possibly the first time. It was normal to expect that, having reached his sixties, he would now be able to live out his life in peace.

Destiny, which Voltaire had so often called into question, intruded brusquely to disrupt his serenity. On November 24, 1755, three weeks after the earthquake in Lisbon, Voltaire received word of the holocaust, which had destroyed countless properties and killed thousands of persons, including many who were in church at the time. The black mood of despair and pessimism occasioned by this senseless destruction set off a revolt against the prevailing philosophy of optimism, with its blind belief in a divine Providence. Many factors, several of them personal, had prepared the ground for the explosive refutation of Providence and the pessimism in "Poème sur le désastre de Lisbonne" ("Poem on the Lisbon Disaster"). He had lost his beloved Emilie; Louis XV had in effect encouraged him to leave his native land; his stay at Potsdam had been disillusioning, and Frederick's "betrayal" of the philosophic cause had shattered his last hope for an enlightened monarch. After his expulsion from Prussia, he felt unwanted and unloved, and Voltaire more than most people needed to be reassured that he was loved and appreciated. The reunion with Mme. Denis, however happy it may have been at first, must have soon soured, if the description of her person and character are at all reliable. She may very well have served as a model for Cunégonde, just as Voltaire's disappointment and necessary adjustment paralleled those of Candide.

The Lisbon earthquake seemed to underscore the futility of man's efforts to create a measure of security and peace. The existence of evil in the world even extended to spheres completely beyond man's control. Fired by his dark mood and rebellion, he quickly wrote "Poème sur le désastre de Lisbonne" and published it in 1756 along with the "Poème sur la Loi Naturelle," which had been composed a few years earlier. This was an odd combination, for the Lisbon poem, even with the more optimistic ending advised by his friends, was essentially a pessimistic work, whereas the "Loi Naturelle," written to counteract the possible evil influence of La Mettrie on Frederick II, was on the whole constructive and optimistic. Jean-Jacques Rousseau, to whom Voltaire sent both works, pointed this out in his famous *Lettre sur la Providence* (*Letter on Providence*, 1756), in which he accepted the "Loi Naturelle" and rejected the Lisbon poem. Rousseau found it absurd that Voltaire, who was wealthy, happy, and universally admired, comdemned Providence, while he himself—impoverished, unknown, and in ill health—defended it. Rousseau failed to appreciate that Voltaire deserved praise, not censure, precisely because he could disregard his own blessings and share the suffering of those less fortunate. It was Rousseau's position that was the selfish one, for it implied that, in view of his own misfortunes, the suffering of others was not as unjust as it appeared to Voltaire and therefore could be accepted with equanimity. Seeing these things as the expression of God's will and essential to the divine pattern of things scarcely made such imperturbability in the face of human misery more attractive.

The exchange with Rousseau precipitated a quarrel that eventually led to a complete break. Their philosophic friendship was severely strained when Rousseau attacked d'Alembert's article on the establishment of a theater in

Geneva. The article, which appeared in Volume VII of the *Encyclopédie* (*Encyclopedia*) in 1757, was believed to have been inspired by Voltaire, with whom d'Alembert had spent five weeks at Les Délices in 1756. Some even credited Voltaire with having written certain parts of it. Rousseau's eloquent but hardly well thought out reply was *Lettre à d'Alembert sur les spectacles* (*Letter to d'Alembert on the Theater*, 1758), a bitter attack on every form of the theater. Voltaire, the great dramatist and amateur actor, felt that Rousseau had really deserted the philosophical camp, for Voltaire and the *philosophes* considered the theater to be a civilizing and beneficial force rather than a detriment to morality. A further estrangement was effected when Rousseau saw in *Candide* (1759) an attack upon him and the long-awaited answer to his *Lettre sur la Providence*. The final break came after the publication in 1762 of *Emile* and the *Contrat social* (*Social Contract*), which Rousseau had imprudently signed. The books were condemned and Rousseau was forced to flee. The paranoiac Rousseau suspected the machinations of Voltaire, and in his *Lettres de la montagne* (*Letters from the Mountains*, 1764), Rousseau's reply to Tronchin's *Lettres de la campagne* (*Letters from the Country*, 1764), he proceeded to expose Voltaire as the author of the audacious *Sermon des cinquante*. Voltaire found this betrayal by a fellow Encyclopedist unpardonable and he retaliated viciously in his *Sentiment des citoyens* (*Sentiments of Citizens*, 1764). D'Alembert and others were dismayed, for their valiant efforts to reconcile these two giants had collapsed. In this instance, as in many others, the effectiveness of Voltaire's retaliation obscured the fact that he was in fact the injured party. This is also exemplified in his quarrel with La Beaumelle over the latter's unauthorized publication of the *Siècle de Louis XIV*. Voltaire replied with *Supplément au Siècle de Louis XIV*, and the battle grew bitter, with Voltaire's superior skill and unyielding vindictiveness carrying the field. Here too the immoderateness of Voltaire's attacks caused the public to forget that the initial fault lay with his adversary.

It is easy to judge Voltaire as ruthless, vindictive, cowardly, and unprincipled. It is even easier for the partisans of Rousseau, who can see only merit in Rousseau's inconsistencies and contradictions, to perceive high principle in his insistence upon signing his works and to mistake for virtue the masochistic posturing of a sick mind and body. Any close scrutiny of Voltaire's life will reveal his persevering struggle to establish a system of justice and universal morality that was to be based on the uniform instincts and desires of man. His correspondence and actions testify to the respect he held for friendship, and continued to hold in the face of betrayal and ingratitude. The names of Desfontaines and Thieriot immediately come to mind. The former, whose life Voltaire saved and whom he twice kept out of prison, repaid his benefactor by publishing the infamous *Voltairomanie* in 1739. Thieriot's treacheries were more numerous but less scandalous. An account of the good deeds Voltaire performed for friends would be endless. The finest accolade to Voltaire's capacity for unselfish action was paid by the person (some say it was Mme. Fréron herself) who wrote to him after the death of his archenemy Fréron, asking Voltaire to take care of the daughter.

As for cowardice, one should remember that conditions in the eighteenth century called for anonymity or pseudonymity if one wished to continue one's battle against the forces of oppression. The very example of Rousseau proved the unwisdom of heedlessly ignoring this elementary fact. Absolute moralists may deplore the enormity of the lies Voltaire told in denying his own works, but he felt that lying was necessary if he wished to continue his usefulness to humanity. He was not above putting in a stock of holy water to escape being burned, Voltaire quipped, by way of explaining to d'Alembert actions that often appeared to be reversals of principles. "My dear friends," he once wrote Damilaville, "if I had a hundred thousand men, I know what I would do; not having them, I shall receive Communion at Easter and you can call me a hypocrite if you wish" [Best. 8858]. At other times he shocked his confreres by referring to Catherine the Great's complicity in the killing of her husband Peter as a mere bagatelle or family quarrel, simply because he admired the achievements of Catherine, who returned the admiration unstintingly. Voltaire was equally capable of refusing to renounce the scoundrel Palissot, who attacked the Encyclopedists in his play, *Les Philosophes;* his grounds were that Palissot was an old friend.

The Lisbon earthquake had awakened the humanitarian; the innumerable examples of flagrant injustice and cruelty that came to his attention in rapid succession after the earthquake transformed him into an inferno of indignation. The battle on behalf of human dignity and justice was henceforth joined, with a sustained dedication unmatched by any other literary figure then or since. His deep and sincere feeling for humanity made no other course possible. He could not be satisfied, Voltaire complained, merely to display wit and, in cowardly fashion, live for himself, as Fontenelle had done. Nor could he be content, like Rousseau, to withdraw from the fray entirely, as though the "Cause" were not in jeopardy. He sent out appeal after appeal to like-minded writers to form a colony to eradicate intolerance and persecution once and for all.

In the meantime, he waged the good fight single-handedly. In 1759, by paying the debts of the six Crassy brothers, he managed to retrieve their heritage from the Jesuits of Ornex. With the Calas affair, the legend of Voltaire as the great humanitarian received its strongest impetus. His fame thereafter increased with each new crusade, to such an extent that "many of the best Christians in Geneva expressed their wonder whether in the presence of the Sovereign Judge their faith would balance the works of this impious man." [9] When the news reached Voltaire on March 22, 1762 that Jean Calas had been cruelly tortured and killed for supposedly having murdered his son in order to prevent his conversion to Catholicism, he immediately started an investigation of the facts, in order to ascertain the innocence of the victim. Once convinced, he set out upon the seemingly hopeless campaign to reverse the decision of the Toulouse court. He was prodigal of both time and money. Every conceivable person, from crowned head to the most obscure Parisian, was exhorted to rally to the cause. Success finally crowned his efforts, almost three years to the day after the execution of Calas. Alas, no sooner did things appear promising in one direction than another case would become public. The Sirvens, mother and father, were condemned in 1764 for having killed their

Huguenot daughter. This time the condemned pair escaped, and Voltaire's successful rehabilitation of them in 1771 had a happier ending. Meanwhile, the Chevalier de La Barre in 1765 had been crucified and mutilated for having failed to remove his cap during a religious procession, singing impious songs, reciting verses of *La Pucelle* (Voltaire's travesty of Chapelain's epic on Joan of Arc), and possessing a copy of Voltaire's *Dictionnaire philosophique*, which was burned with him. This last caused Voltaire such a fright that his friends feared for his sanity. When reason had regained control, he courageously undertook the fight to vindicate La Barre, this time without success, though he did manage to place d'Etallonde, La Barre's companion, in Prussia, safely beyond the reach of the authorities. The last well-known instance of Voltaire's humanitarian undertakings concerned Count Lally, who was decapitated on May 6, 1766. The news of Lally's rehabilitation reached Voltaire in 1778 just in time to add a note of joy to the grim aspect of death. In addition to these inspiring battles, Voltaire waged many others that were equally important from the point of view of justice and humanity, although not so well known today.

Comparisons tend to be invidious: one critic may assert that Voltaire's smile accomplished more than Rousseau's tears; another may prefer the sublime although often turgid eloquence of Rousseau to Voltaire's much vaunted lucidity and brevity; some find Diderot more profound as an intellect and as a scientific spirit; still others favor Montesquieu's contribution, both for the literary merit of his *Lettres persanes* (*Persian Letters*, 1721) and for the scientific scope of *De l'Esprit des lois* (*Spirit of Laws*, 1748). One thing hardly seems debatable; that is, if one figure had to be chosen as perhaps the most representative of the eighteenth century as a whole, it would be Voltaire, so well did he personify the disparate elements that made up the century. The eighteenth century was one of unrest and increasing bourgeois criticism, exemplified by Beaumarchais' plays, in which one often sees the Revolution prefigured. Despite his conservative and monarchical tendencies, his change of name to de Voltaire, and his earlier years spent as a courtier, no one represented the critical bourgeois better than

Voltaire. If the purpose of the Revolution was primarily to overthrow the forces of injustice and tyranny, certainly no man was more responsible for the initial phases of this struggle than was Voltaire, whose entire life and work was aimed at the restoration of man's dignity and human rights. The eighteenth century was also a century of religious change, during which the authority of the Church was constantly being subjected to examination. Did any man contribute more to the weakening of the Church? The deification of Reason by the revolutionaries must in large part be traced back to its roots in Voltaire's deliberate undermining of miracles, dogmas, and revelations.

Another aspect of the century was its classical spirit. Voltaire's severest detractor could not deny him the distinction of having been the greatest classicist of his time. Wherever one's sympathies may lie in the quarrel between Voltaire and Rousseau, the fact is that Voltaire could never have admired Rousseau precisely because of the latter's unclassical style. Neither the beautifully lyrical and eloquent language of the *Nouvelle Héloise* (*New Heloise*, 1761) nor the imprecision of *Emile* and the *Contrat social* could have appealed to Voltaire, so committed was he to classical principles. That Voltaire could speak well of Rousseau at all was a tribute to the former's conviction that a bond of fraternity should unite all the *philosophes* who opposed the forces of oppression. Similarly, Voltaire was prepared to sacrifice literary principles and overlook differences in religious and esthetic beliefs in his support and defense of Diderot, who "in theory, at least, was a much more dangerous opponent of the classical ideal than was Rousseau—in literature a pronounced and romantic apologist of the strong emotions and of Shakespeare, in philosophy and religion a materialist and atheist." [10]

So intent was Voltaire on establishing a practical morality for mankind that he often, and not always consciously, kept his own philosophical views in check in order to avoid the disastrous moral consequences that were possible from a misunderstanding or misapplication by the masses of his philosophical determinism. A *philosophe*, he was persuaded, could safely dispense with the moral guidance offered by religion; for the common man, Voltaire preferred the greater assurance afforded by religion. One could charge him with hypocrisy, but it was hypocrisy employed for noble ends: "He is realistically, not cynically, opportunistic. His ends, which he knows must be approached gradually if at all, justify many, not any, means." [11] It was this fear of moral consequences that dictated his outright opposition to the adamant materialism and atheism of some *philosophes*. Actually Voltaire's admiration and recognition of an intelligence behind the vast forces of the universe impelled him to seek a rational proof of the necessity of God as a first cause, and prevented him from traveling the full route to the atheism that was explicit in La Mettrie's *Homme machine* (*Man Machine*, 1747) and d'Holbach's *Système de la nature* (*System of Nature*, 1770), and implicit in Diderot's *Pensées philosophiques* (*Philosophical Thoughts*, 1746).

The mystery of the universe always fascinated and haunted Voltaire; this fascination is best revealed in the article "Religion" in the *Dictionnaire philosophique*. True, his mysticism was divorced from creed and consequently quite different from that of the religious mystics, whose greatest crime, in Voltaire's eyes, was to mistake their visions for truths. Nor was he inclined in the slightest to withdraw from human realities on the wings of metaphysical meditation. The sensationalistic epistemology and psychology of Locke were ever ready to harness whatever mystical flights Newtonian discoveries may have inspired. Moreover, he insisted at all times upon a return to the central problem of man, that of moral philosophy; all problems of good and evil had to be weighed against a scale of social rather than religious values.

Voltaire achieved his humanitarian results by refusing to allow his age the luxury of overlooking crimes committed in the name of justice or religion. During his last twenty years, when he inundated the land with letters and articles designed to dispel public apathy, Voltaire was in a real sense a magnificent journalist and pamphleteer. Yet all his efforts as a reformer, notable and worthy as they were, occurred in the twilight of an illustrious career of letters. And the literary twilight also produced works of sufficient literary importance to rival the good works of the "Don Quixote of the condemned and tortured" of the Ferney years. These publications included: "Traité sur la tolérance" ("Treatise on Tolerance," 1763); *Dictionnaire philosophique* (1764); *Le Philosophe ignorant (The Ignorant Philosopher*, 1766); *Siècle de Louis XV (Age of Louis XV*, 1763–1768); *L'Ingénu (The Huron*, 1767); and in 1772, the result of two years' work, *Les Questions sur l'Encyclopédie (Questions on the Encyclopedia*), the 378 articles of which more boldly strengthen the positions taken by Diderot in the *Encyclopédie*—not to mention the innumerable minor works which added to his fame as the arch-mocker and blasphemer of all time. When one adds the impressive list of works written before the Ferney period, some of which are incontestably masterpieces, it is manifestly a distortion of the true value of Voltaire to say, as Paul Valéry did at the commemoration of the 250th anniversary of Voltaire: "If he had died at age 60, he would at present be virtually forgotten, and we would not be solemnly gathered here to render homage to the author of *Mérope, Zaïre* and *La Henriade*." [12] If they would not have assembled to honor the author of the works mentioned by Valéry, the chances are excellent that a similar assemblage would have gathered to honor the author of *Lettres philosophiques*, "Le Mondain," *Mahomet, Zadig, Siècle de Louis XIV, Essai sur les moeurs, Dictionnaire philosophique*, and the truly incomparable correspondence of over 20,000 letters that makes the whole century come to life.*

Voltaire's genius and his rank as one of the greatest and most cosmopolitan writers France ever produced must be justified by his intellectual works, not by his humanitarian deeds. The impact of his ideas has helped to set a direction for human behavior; the precision and clarity of his writings have set the standard for those qualities that have become the trademark of the French language and given meaning to Antoine Rivarol's statement: "What is not clear is not French." There is some justification in re-

---

* A true picture of Voltaire's development and career as a writer necessitates a knowledge of the dates when he wrote his works, for often ten to twelve years, sometimes more, separated composition and publication; cf. p. ix of Ira O. Wade's *Voltaire's Micromégas: A Study in the Fusion of Science, Myth and Art* (Princeton: Univ. Press, 1950).

garding Voltaire's life as his most laudable achievement, so earnestly did he seek and so well did he formulate the basis for a workable ethic that could give meaning and happiness to man during his short tenure on earth. But the indisputable genius of Voltaire should not be obscured by that life, full and rich enough almost to give one a feeling of vertigo. The Voltaire who will continue to live long after his humanitarian deeds have been forgotten must be sought in the author of imperishable masterpieces and the master of literary style.

CHAPTER II

VOLTAIRE'S

PHILOSOPHICAL TALES

AND STYLE

*T*he traditional notion, which is difficult to combat, is that Voltaire was just a propagandist, a skillful popularizer of the philosophical ideas of others. The repetitive quality of his work, whatever the genre, unfortunately contributes to the erroneous conclusion that Voltaire was not a thinker and writer of outstanding merit. For his own century he was unquestionably France's greatest poet and dramatist, and with the possible exception of Montesquieu, the greatest historian. Changing tastes have revised these evaluations, with the result that, since the nineteenth century, the lasting claim to literary fame of the once celebrated author of *La Henriade* and rival of Corneille and Racine rests ironically upon the philosophical tales that he wrote when he was well past middle age.

A writer must be judged on both form and content. Emphasis on ideas alone would justify the epithet of propagandist or popularizer and vitiate the writer's title to literary immortality; emphasis on style alone would be as meaningless, Voltaire would probably agree, as an attempt by a well-dressed mannequin to replace man in society. Voltaire happily combined both in everything he wrote, with greater felicity in some genres than in others. It is generally conceded by most critics today that the highest form of his literary art, the most effective combination of the moralist of genius and the gifted prose artist, can be found in his tales. A born writer, endowed with an infallible sense of style, he would have been virtually incapable of writing anything very badly, either in poetry or prose, so rigorously did he seek in both the same purity and precision. The voluminous correspondence, the definitive and scholarly edition of which has been published at Les Délices by Theodore Besterman, attests to Voltaire's instinctive gift for the right phrase and his superlative command of language. To be sure, modern tastes have relegated his poetry to a position of relative unimportance; most critics summarily dismiss it as undeserving of serious study. Yet the poetic skills that captivated generations of Europeans are still there, and future critics who are bold enough to defy the rigidly established tradition of his unworthiness as a poet may some day succeed in rehabilitating the poetic Voltaire.

The two greatest French writers of the eighteenth century were Voltaire and Rousseau. Personal taste will dictate one's preference, and their diametrically opposed styles and ideas will simplify the choice. Those who prefer the intellectual appeal made through pungent satire, irony, and caricature will unhesitatingly select Voltaire; the admirers of a rhetorical and melodious style will immediately choose Rousseau. Each in his own way achieved a literary perfection unequaled in his own time, and rarely matched since.

To a great extent it is the attraction of the man and his philosophy of life that will determine the reader's allegiance, and their differences in these respects were as striking as their styles. Voltaire, the practical moralist and realist, by nature an extrovert and gregarious, represented the triumph of reason over sentiment and of action over theory. Rousseau, in part because of maladies more physically real than those of Voltaire, was withdrawn and at ease only when he was alone or with intimate friends. It is consequently natural to find Rousseau constantly probing the inner world of Rousseau, whereas Voltaire was so preoccupied with the world around him that he was never able to finish either his *Mémoires* (*Memoirs*) which he started in 1758, or an autobiography that he began in 1776. He found it simply ludicrous to occupy his time thinking and writing of himself. Apparently this also extended to members of his family, for in spite of the mountainous correspondence, very little is learned about his sister, his brother, or his father.

The twentieth century, with its obsession for Freud and the psychiatric couch, has taken Rousseau more and more to its bosom; because of his very lucidity, Voltaire's fame has suffered in an age that equates obscurity with profundity. "The time has come to treat with more seriousness the work of the man who," in Ira Wade's opinion, "best expresses the multiple cultural achievements of the eighteenth century." [1] And in compliance with the present scale of values, this discussion of Voltaire's literary works will consider only those that are generally agreed to be the best of each genre, in the following order of importance attributed to the genres by twentieth-century critics: (1) philosophical tales, (2) history, (3) drama, and (4) poetry. In this chapter an examination of four *contes: Zadig, Micromégas, Candide,* and *L'Ingénu* will be followed by a general study of Voltaire's prose style.

It should be stated at the outset that Voltaire's philosophical viewpoint in the tales does not differ greatly from that expressed in his other works, although of course with the passage of time his attacks became more comprehensive and forthright. The "Epître à Uranie" had already presented unequivocally his deistic ideas, and certainly the *Lettres philosophiques* in 1734 indirectly or directly attacked most of the political, social, and religious evils exposed in the tales. The success of the narrative form, attested to by the numerous editions of *Candide* and Voltaire's repeated use of this genre, corroborates the theory that a new artistic form was needed to replace the epic and tragedy, which had disintegrated or at least no longer served as adequate vehicles for the new content of the second half of the eighteenth century.

Voltaire's first attempt at the *conte* form dates back to 1739 with the *Voyages du baron de Gangan* (*Baron de*

Gangan's Travels), known to us only through the correspondence with Frederick II, to whom Voltaire had sent it
in June 1739. In spite of the risk involved in taking Voltaire at his word—so accustomed was he to camouflaging,
distorting, or simply by reverse snobbery belittling his own
works—one can assume that this first venture was literally,
as he explained to Frederick in his letter of June 20, 1739,
"a philosophic trifle that should be read as relaxation after
more serious work" [Best. 1934]. Voltaire, being a delightful if disconcerting mixture of the serious and frivolous,
enjoyed diverting himself and his friends by writing trivial
or often pornographic works like *La Pucelle*. The *Voyages
de Gangan* was very likely in this vein, although more philosophical, as he himself suggested. In his reply of July 7,
1739 [Best. 1944], Frederick described Gangan as "a celestial traveler," thus giving rise to the speculation that this
may have been a preliminary version of *Micromégas*.[2]

Zadig substantiates the view held by Norman L. Torrey
that "Voltaire's tales have a way of summing up certain
periods of his existence and certain problems with which he
was then faced."[3] Written in 1747, only a short time after
many honors had been showered upon him, it pointedly
reflects Voltaire's increasing concern with the ominous
clouds gathering around his head after the incident of the
jeu de la reine. The realization that the danger of persecution was ever present, even when a person was the object of
praise and adulation, definitely dampened the relative complacency of Voltaire's courtier years during the mid-forties.
The doubt and pessimism that became firmly entrenched
during the fifties was already replacing the exuberant optimism of the late thirties. No longer could Voltaire accept
the *tout est bien* philosophy stoutly supported in "Le Mondain," and like his alter ego, Zadig, he began to question
more and more the beneficent ways of Providence. Destiny
took curious turns; tragically, it often depended on the un-
predictable actions of prejudiced men. Voltaire points up
the capriciousness of destiny by having Zadig's life saved by
the royal parrot. Then when all seemed hopeful again, as it
did for Voltaire in the forties, Zadig, the new Prime Minister of King Moabdar, sees all his honors and rewards vanish

before a new wave of misfortune, and like Voltaire is forced to flee.

In writing the philosophical tales, Voltaire, freed from the restraints imposed by the established classical genres, could give free rein to his natural instinct for satire, burlesque, and parody. He possessed the talents and the genius that were ideally suited to the *conte* form: "a clear and concise style, a powerful and flashing wit, a sense of action and dialogue, and an imagination which, though somewhat at sea in the realms of feeling, was completely at home in the sphere of ideas." [4] Not a novel in the proper sense of the word, since it lacks character development and plot, the philosophical tale is concerned primarily with the dramatic presentation of ideas. It is "a fictitious prose narrative wherein theme molds all the other component elements (action, character, setting, diction, etc.) into a stylized, two-dimensional, emotionally sublimated demonstration." [5] The frequent use of crisp dialogue supplies the dramatic punch to the narrative; the tyrannical omnipresence and omnipotence of the author's ego carries the ideational theme. On the surface the reader is presented with a series of frivolous and humorous adventures of the hero, but Voltaire preeminently fulfilled Condorcet's formula for writing a successful *conte:* "One must be philosophical without appearing to be so." [6] In the dedicatory epistle to *Zadig,* Voltaire specifically warned the reader that the work contained more than was apparent to the eye.

ZADIG

The piquancy of Voltaire's prose style in this new narrative genre added a further dimension of effectiveness unparalleled in his other works. And the excellence of *Zadig,* his first full-blown venture in the *conte* form, gives the lie to the contention that Voltaire kept on improving in this genre until he reached the ultimate perfection of *Candide.* For some critics, *Zadig* incorporates greater conciseness than *Candide,* without sacrificing any of the latter's variety.

Certainly one can virtually say of Voltaire at the time of his writing *Zadig* what George Havens claimed for him when he wrote *Candide*: "His intellectual development was complete; his style was formed; Voltaire was at the height of his powers, ready to produce the masterpiece which in its kind has never been surpassed or even equalled." [7] There is no doubt that Voltaire had found the most appropriate form for his particular talents.

In *Zadig* all the familiar ills of society are laid bare in his treatment of: medicine, justice, venality, religious intolerance and persecution, women, love, superstition, prejudice of any kind, slavery, and especially Providence. Brief samplings of Voltaire's thrusts at the injustices he found about him will reveal the method of his attacks and the stylistic skills he employed for their most effective exposure. With a few words he delivers himself of his low opinion of man in general: Zadig possessed "great riches, and consequently many friends" [XXI:33]. A frequent butt of Voltaire's satire was quackery in medicine. After Zadig was wounded in defending Sémire, a doctor was called. The great Hermès came with a large entourage.

He visited the patient, and declared that he would lose his eye; he even predicted the day and hour when this fateful accident would occur. "If it had been the right eye," he said, "I would have cured him; but the wounds of the left eye are incurable. . . ." Two days later, the abscess burst by itself. Zadig was cured. Hermès wrote a book in which he proved that he should not have been cured. Zadig did not read it [XXI:34].

Women always appeared in an unfavorable light. Romantic love is cynically dismissed by this man who has clearly never experienced love. The Pimpette affair was merely an adolescent crush; his liaison with Emilie was definitely not romantic love, and his other liaisons, including that with his niece, were plainly physical relationships. In *Zadig*, all the women fare badly. Sémire abandoned Zadig once his wound was declared incurable, and Azora, "the best-behaved and best-born of the city," easily succumbed to the ruse engineered by Zadig and Cador. By her readiness to cut off Zadig's nose in order to heal her new lover Cador, she too displayed the feminine weaknesses of infidelity and inconstancy. Astarté herself is not spared; she does after all transfer her love from Moabdar, her husband and king, to Zadig. The most striking example is Missouf, the capricious one, although by implication the scores of women who flocked to consult Zadig because of his physical attraction were equally flighty and frivolous.

Injustice that emanated from the courts was by far the worst, since theoretically they should be protecting the rights of man. The memorable example in *Zadig* is the famous incident of Zadig's trial for supposedly having stolen the king's horse and the queen's dog. He was quickly judged and convicted. After the animals were discovered, the judges found themselves in the "painful necessity of having to modify their judgment" [XXI:38]. Proved innocent, Zadig had only to pay heavy fines before being given the privilege of addressing the judges, the "pillars of justice, founts of knowledge, mirrors of truth" [XXI:38]. Superstition and prejudice were favorite targets of Voltaire's ire. While in Sétoc's service, Zadig exposed the foolishness of worshipping the creations of God instead of God, by prostrating himself before the lighted candles just as Sétoc had done before the stars. Skillfully employing his knowledge of human psychology, Zadig also put an end to the inhuman custom that compelled widows to perish on the funeral pyres of their husbands. To counter the argument that this ancient practice had become hallowed through long usage, Zadig replied that reason was more ancient. Because of his intervention, a law was passed that prevented any widow from destroying herself without first having spent an hour in private with a young man. From that day forth, no woman sacrificed herself either for love of her husband or to conform to what had previously been sacred custom.

The most telling criticism of religious intolerance came in the apologue, "Le Souper," in which the fanaticism behind religious quarrels was exposed in order to demonstrate the superiority of deism. By convincing each disputant that, regardless of differing practices and dogmas, they all worshipped one and the same God, Zadig reconciled their differences. Humanity and justice were the touchstones of

Voltaire's philosophy. It was natural then to find occasional indictments of slavery in his works, for nothing more effectively degraded the human being and destroyed one's dignity. The treatment of the subject in *Zadig*, nevertheless, is too light to constitute an effective denunciation of slavery. Like Montesquieu, who has a delightfully ironic indictment of slavery in the *Lettres persanes*, he actually owned shares in a company that trafficked in the slave trade. Voltaire would no doubt have dismissed this discrepancy lightly with the observation that business was business, and that if he did not profit, someone else would. Or he might have said, as he did in *Essai sur les moeurs*, that "a people that sells its own children is more culpable than the buyer; this trade reveals our superiority; the person who takes on a master was born to have one" [XIII: 177–178]. Neither the behavior nor the justification seems laudable; one can only say in defense of Voltaire that if the continuance of slavery had depended solely on his participation, it would have ceased abruptly, regardless of profit. Perhaps the twentieth-century person who is ready to condemn Voltaire should keep in mind that conditions in the eighteenth century condoned the existence of servants and slaves. One will recall that Voltaire apparently did not feel they were out of place, even in the ideal human setting of Eldorado.

Destiny and the existence of wrongdoing in the world constitute the central themes of *Zadig*. The book of destiny, which is also featured in *Micromégas*, was being read by the venerable, white-bearded Hermit when the curious Zadig encountered him. And just as in *Micromégas*, the message of the book was indecipherable. Our hero had reached the point where the arguments of philosophers had become unacceptable, in the light of a concatenation of misfortunes that was capped by Itobad's theft of his white armor, without which he was unable to proclaim himself the victor of the tournament and thus claim Astarté. Throughout the series of episodes shared with the hermit, reason and human conscience are seen at work in this early revolt against the *tout est bien* of philosophical optimism. Yet so skillfully did Voltaire handle the subject that many readers accepted his position as compatible with orthodoxy —including Rousseau, to judge from his *Lettre sur la Prov-*

idence. Voltaire's message is clear—it can be seen in Zadig's insistent and unanswered "but" to the Hermit's demands for unquestioning submission. The full implication of the "but" in *Zadig* emerges when compared with Voltaire's letter of Nov. 6, 1750 to his niece, Mme. Denis. Writing from Potsdam, where the honeymoon period had already changed to "absinthe"—to borrow the terminology of *Zadig*—Voltaire was describing the apparently happy life with Frederick II, while at the same time guardedly expressing his reservations by the insertion of "but":

> The suppers of the king are delicious, one finds a display of reason, wit, learning; liberty reigns there; he [Frederick] is the soul of all that; no bad humor, no clouds of dissension, at least no storms. My life is free and a busy one; but . . . but. . . . Operas, comedies, carrousels, suppers at Sans-Souci, military drills, concerts, studies, readings; but . . . but. . . . The city of Berlin, big, better laid out than Paris, palaces, theatres, affable queens, charming princesses, beautiful and shapely ladies in waiting, the home of Mme. de Tyrconel always filled and often too crowded; but . . . but . . . , my dear child, the weather promises to become quite cold [Best. 3683].

MICROMEGAS

Micromégas in 1752 presents a more thorough treatment of man's relative role in the universe and of the vanity of metaphysical speculation and systems. Voltaire was deliberately undermining what he felt to be basic assumptions of the Church—namely, that God had created man in His image; that man represented His greatest creation; and that therefore the universe was created for man. Instead, Voltaire insisted, man's place was in the regular zoological chain, even though he was a superior animal endowed with reasoning processes that far outstripped those of other animals. In other words, the famous dichotomy of Descartes was rejected. Scientific progress, represented by the work of Copernicus, Galileo, Newton, and others, Voltaire argued, reduced the importance attached to man and to the earth. During the interrogation of the humans on board

ship by Micromégas and the Saturnian, the disciple of
Locke proclaimed the supremacy of the senses and acknowledged his ignorance before the unknowable. By
contrast, "l'animalcule en bonnet carré," representing the
Church, claimed to know all and declared that all truth
could be found in St. Thomas Aquinas, who assured the
believers that "all was made uniquely for man" [XXI:122].
This statement elicited the Homeric laughter of Micromégas and the Saturnian, causing the ship to fall
into the latter's pocket. The whole discussion between the
giants and the humans was designed to mock the insuffer-
able vanity of man and the incessant quarreling among men
who had become embittered by religious and political
differences. The too frequent result of such bickering was
war, and no justification of war was possible. Its senseless
carnage could never be rationalized by jurisdictional rights
over "a mound of mud" and less so by the desire to impose
one's religious dogmas upon others. Voltaire never tired of
saying that those engaged in the murder that was legiti-
mized by war scarcely ever knew what they were fighting
about. The last chapter of *Micromégas* demonstrates this,
but a more effective case was made in *Le Monde comme il
va,* when Babouc tries in vain to find anyone who is able to
explain the reasons for his bellicose actions.

The end of the tale delivers the final thrust at metaphysical pretensions and at the vanity of speculating upon problems that are insoluble by man's finite mind. The Sirian
could produce only a blank book in answer to the questions
posed by the humans, in spite of his more numerous senses,
and his greater wisdom, experience, and size. Certainly,
Voltaire implies, there can be little hope for puny man to
succeed where the Sirian had failed. Voltaire would counsel us to devote our energies and intelligence to problems
that are susceptible of solution through observable and demonstrable evidence, and thereby to improve, by however
little, the all too miserable lot of man. This was a recurring
theme in the works of Voltaire; it reflects his preference for
Locke and Newton over Emilie's predilection for the philosophy of Leibnitz, as taught to her by Koenig, who probably served as the prototype for Pangloss. One can surmise
that Voltaire's denunciation of Leibnitzian jargon might

well have been stronger were it not for Emilie's enthusiasm and admiration.

Philosophical terminology was anathema to Voltaire. He carried his demands for lucidity of expression and practicality almost to the point of irrationality. Most pure speculation was deemed to be useless, or worse still, potentially harmful, because self-centered and ambitious persons—priests and laymen alike—could and did easily distort and misapply that type of language for selfish purposes. Practical reasons were then in part responsible for his incessant warfare on metaphysics. For example, during the discussion in *Micromégas* between the giants and the passengers of the ship, Voltaire scoffed at the follower of Leibnitz who described the soul as "a needle that shows the hours while my body chimes; or if you wish, it is the soul that chimes while my body points out the hour; or my soul is the mirror of the universe and my body is the border of the mirror." Voltaire cryptically added: "All that is very clear" [XXI:121]. In opposition to this nonsense, the disciple of Locke presented a sensible and modest view based on empirical knowledge derived from the senses. The same reasoning impelled Voltaire to lampoon the innate ideas of Descartes who saw the newborn endowed with a knowledge of God and with metaphysical notions. Voltaire could see no advantage in possessing all these gifts at birth only to lose them with increased maturity and intelligence.

The denigration of Descartes in *Micromégas* tends to support the argument for an earlier publication date than has been usually assigned to it. The views expressed are more consonant with those found in the *Lettres philosophiques* than with the mellowed position of later years, when Voltaire saw the good in Descartes as at least balancing the bad. Nor did *Micromégas* sufficiently reflect the growing pessimism that manifested itself by the early fifties in his letters from Potsdam. Moreover, had *Micromégas* been written around 1752, the reference, at the end of Chapter 4, to Maupertuis' trip to measure a degree of the meridian would in all likelihood have been more caustic, given the rivalry between these two at Potsdam and Voltaire's well-known penchant for excoriating his enemies whenever and wherever the opportunity presented itself.

The kind of satiric attack leveled at Fontenelle at the end of Chapter 1 and the beginning of Chapter 2 would likely have been Maupertuis' lot in 1752. Witness in *Candide* (start of Chapter 22) how Voltaire used the full measure of his satire against Maupertuis in discussing a contest held by the Academy of Sciences to determine why the wool of Candide's rescued sheep was red: "the prize was awarded to a scientist from the North," Voltaire explained, "who demonstrated by means of a formula A plus B, minus C, divided by Z, that the sheep had to be red and would die of sheep-pox" [XXI: 187].

On the whole *Micromégas* does not measure up to *Zadig, Candide,* or *l'Ingénu,* and in its variety of attack does not even equal *Le Monde comme il va.* The narrative flows along with fewer "punch lines" to accentuate the meaning; satire and caricature, in spite of the obvious use of giants to lampoon man's intolerable pretensions, are less in evidence. In short, the style and presentation are not as effective as in *Zadig* or *Candide,* perhaps because almost the whole *conte* was concerned with a more restricted subject, which thereby restricted the possible use of many of the favorite weapons in Voltaire's well-stocked armory.

CANDIDE

➤ By virtual unanimity, *Candide* is judged to be Voltaire's masterpiece. For most critics it qualifies as a classic; William Bottiglia, who has recently undertaken a full-scale study of *Candide,* prefers the classification of miniature classic. The excellence of many of Voltaire's *contes* can be attributed in part to a prose style that is admirably suited to that new literary form; the pre-eminence of *Candide* finds its justification in the most felicitous marriage of style and content. "It is quickened and deepened by the energy of Voltaire's personality, the momentous vivacity of its stylistic movement, the philosophic sympathy it arouses for its message, and the levels of meaning it suggests through a unique fusion of irony, symbolism, and, here and there, duplicity." [8]

By 1758, what Morize called the Leibnitzian chain of

causes was complete. The Voltaire who had begun to show definite hostility to the confusing philosophy of Leibnitz in the late thirties and early forties, had reached the bottom of his emotional curve by 1749, according to Norman Torrey, and was openly challenging the "best of all possible worlds" in *Zadig*. The former admirer of Alexander Pope's *Essay on Man* (1733), who had paid Pope the homage of imitation in his seven "Discours en vers sur l'Homme" in 1738 and 1739, had become convinced of the absurdity of "Whatever is, is right." In *Zadig*, the message of the angel Jesrad closely resembled Pope's faith in Providence and his optimism: "there is no evil of which good is not born, there is no such thing as Chance; all is trial, punishment, recompense or foresight." And Jesrad concludes with this advice to Zadig: "Weak mortal, stop disputing that which you should adore" [XXI:90]. Pope had preached the same message at the end of his first epistle:

> *All Nature is but Art, unknown to thee;*
> *All Chance, Direction, which thou canst not see;*
> *All Discord, Harmony not understood;*
> *All partial Evil, universal Good;*
> *And, spite of Pride, in erring Reason's spite,*
> *One truth is clear,* WHATEVER IS, IS RIGHT.[9]

By 1748, with the publication of *Le Monde comme il va*, the feeble remonstrance of Zadig against the "Whatever is, is right" philosophy of Jesrad had become an open acceptance and recognition of evil. On the basis of Babouc's report, Ituriel spared Persépolis with the observation:: "If all is not well, all is bearable" [XXI:16].

Whether *Candide* reflects pessimism in the philosophical sense of the word, or simply despair at existing circumstances, there can be little doubt about the increasing dismay with which Voltaire viewed the human condition. The "garden" of *Candide* undoubtedly conveys a measure of optimism, but it does not entirely dispel the aura of pessimism that permeates the otherwise uninspiring, even discouraging atmosphere. And this is as it should be, given the main themes of *Candide*: the connection between human conduct and the presence of evil in the world, and the reduction to absurdity of the philosophical optimism of Pope,

Leibnitz, and their defender, Rousseau. The survey of the world's ills is made possible by the experiences and adventures of the hero Candide. Essentially, he is naive, sincere, and well-intentioned, but he is hopelessly indoctrinated with the philosophy of his master Pangloss. After each disillusionment Candide remains filled with hope, persistently mouthing Pangloss's Leibnitzian phrases, ever hopeful that the realization of his dreams is just around the proverbial corner. Ironically, when Candide reaches Eldorado, in essence "the ideal of human aspiration," he is driven out, in Lester Crocker's words, by the "dynamism of his vices." This is one aspect of Voltaire's pessimistic commentary on life. Man by his very nature must strive for goals; therefore a life of perfection would in the long run become intolerable, downright unlivable, for without objectives ambition would disappear and man would vegetate. Or, as in the case of the Troglodytes in Montesquieu's *Lettres persanes*, the burden of a virtuous life would become too heavy for imperfect man to endure. Indirectly, Voltaire is probably presenting a parody and caricature of the Garden of Eden and Original Sin.

Vanity and woman are the reasons given for Candide's departure from Eldorado. The human desire to stand out over one's fellowman spurred Candide to leave with a supply of diamonds, which were meaningless in Eldorado because of their commonness, yet were capable elsewhere of giving him status and even superiority. Cunégonde, symbolizing the eternal woman, was clearly the primary reason for his abandonment of the terrestrial paradise. It is Cunégonde whom Candide was constantly pursuing; Voltaire is in effect preaching the stupidity of chasing dream-bubbles, which always burst when clutched. He emphasizes this point by having Cunégonde turn out to be ugly and waspish. Candide, the faithful and honorable lover, keeps his promise and marries her. The explanation by some critics that the marriage displayed a reversal of Voltaire's antifeminism seems highly implausible. Voltaire rendered Candide's resignation to the unpleasant turn of events somewhat more logical by imbuing the hero with a new-found social consciousness. Still, it was the cynical and antifeminist Voltaire who, with a glint in his eyes, said that

Cunégonde had become a passable pastry cook. Certainly he was enjoying the plight of the husband and lover eternally tied to a cantankerous and ugly woman. Nor was Cunégonde's situation more enviable; she had lost her beauty and was condemned to a loveless marriage. It would be naive to suppose that the consolation derived from the knowledge of her social contribution could compensate entirely for these losses.

— The numerous trials that Candide had to undergo before achieving the spiritual and social awakening which made possible the sensible and practical ethic embodied in the conclusion would seem to indicate the difficulty of attaining this goal. One could normally have expected Candide, newly married to his long-sought Cunégonde and united with his friends, to lead a happy and contented life. Yet this did not happen, for they wasted their time in fruitless speculation, which was devoid of meaningful action. Their socially eroding idleness resulted in a horrible ennui, and the at best helpless Candide, who never did seem to know what course of action to pursue, became more indecisive and immobilized. The only member of the group engaged in constructive work was Cacambo; because he alone worked, however, he cursed his fate. The despair and discontent of Cacambo's "garden" obviously made Cacambo's existence unacceptable as a pattern for society.

The next step involved the Turk's "garden." On the surface all seemed idyllic. With his two sons and daughters the old Turk had created a prosperous farm, which Candide admired. Their dedication to work had successfully eliminated the three common dangers for man: boredom, vice, and need. Nonetheless, Voltaire's ideal was not realized by the Turk, for he eschewed all social responsibility. As a result, there could be little hope for social improvement in a proliferation of similarly self-centered units. By contrast, Candide's "garden" represented a larger group, equally dedicated to useful work and likewise involved at the social level, thereby holding out hope for the future while satisfying the needs of the present. Not that the tinge of pessimism depicted by the "shrinkage" in the Turk's life had completely vanished from Candide's "garden." Pangloss after all remained Pangloss; he was philosophizing to the end, so much so that Martin found it necessary to silence his perpetual flow of talk with advice that closely resembled the Turk's: "Let's work without reasoning; that's the only way to render our life bearable" [XXI:217]. And to a certain degree, Candide himself revealed the lingering element of despair in their lives when, in answer to the old woman's question as to which was preferable—to be subjected to all the misfortunes that had been their lot or to remain there in complete idleness—he replied: "That's a big question" [XXI:215]. The adoption of the work routine did improve the situation deplored by the old woman, yet in spite of the marked "progression from pessimistic drift to meliorism," and the promise now held out by the future, human wickedness with its concomitant miseries had not been eliminated. Voltaire succeeded in pointing out what direction to take; he had likewise focused attention on the human ills to be avoided or cured. Now it remained for man to persevere on the path set by the cooperation and good-will demonstrated by the members of Candide's "garden," and hopefully work toward a better tomorrow. In this respect, despite the reservations noted, "the wisdom of the Conclusion is not narrow and disappointing, but excitingly dynamic, expansive, and challenging at every level of the civilized adventure." [10]

The tremendous scope of *Candide* is an important contribution to the excellence of the work. It presents, as Flaubert maintained, a synthesis of Voltaire's thought. The variety of ideas is greater than in *Zadig*, and they are somewhat more developed. A mere catalogue, albeit incomplete, of the subjects treated in *Candide* suggests the breadth of Voltaire's ideational canvas: pride of rank; court flattery; human greed; medicine; women and romantic love; political and social injustice; corruption of courts and judges; philosophical optimism; Providence; the concept of Free Will; religious intolerance, dogmas, and fanaticism; war, music, art, and literature—in short, virtually every field of human endeavor. The examples of each are legion; a few will suffice to illustrate the Voltairean approach.

Special note should be taken of Voltaire's treatment of war, one of his favorite targets. *Zadig, Babouc,* and *Micromégas* had already leveled attacks against its stupidity and inhumanity. Voltaire particularly deplored the role played by the Church and its representatives. Never did they preach against this crime that combines the most wicked aspects of human conduct: pillage, rape, homicide, and wholesale devastation. "Instead, the good priests solemnly and ceremoniously blessed the standards of the murderers; and their confreres sang, for money, Jewish songs, when the earth was soaked with blood" [XXVII:374]. In *Candide* the "Te Deums" were said in both armies, to give thanks for victory or to stave off defeat (even as they are today). All of Candide's experiences with the Bulgares, after being expelled from the baron's estate in Westphalia, and especially those of Cunégonde and the old woman, highlight the inhuman practices of the "heroic butchery" called war.

Some may become justifiably incensed by the glaring inconsistency between Voltaire's precept and his actions. He made money from the shipping of military supplies, and he tried to sell armored weapons, first to France, later to Catherine the Great. These actions, the full story of which remains unknown, can scarcely erase the overwhelming evidence of Voltaire's continuing hatred of war. (In this connection, it may prove worthwhile to recount an incident that demonstrates the danger of relying on incidental quotations from the author himself, or attempting to construct a philosophy and a life around stories that are not fully known and documented. A graduate student, given to *étalages de science*, one day questioned an eminent professor's interpretation of Voltaire by citing chapter and verse to prove Voltaire had said just the opposite. The professor replied with a smile that combined human understanding and Voltairean irony: "Voltaire may have said exactly what you attribute to him, but, you see, even though he said that, he did not mean it." Just as with the work of Voltaire, the lesson remained long after the smiles had vanished.)

In *Candide* the attacks on religious dogmas, superstition, intolerance, and fanaticism are somewhat commonplace. The barbarity of the Inquisition is pointedly denounced. The inquisitors, Voltaire notifies us in a matter-of-fact way, had discovered an infallible way to prevent the recurrence of earthquakes—the presentation of a beautiful auto-da-fé.

Immediately after one of these entertaining spectacles, "the earth trembled anew and went into a violent upheaval" [XXI:149]. An inquisitor is also used to highlight the immorality of Churchmen; he became the rival of Issachar for Cunégonde's favors. And more piquantly and maliciously, Voltaire has the old woman reveal, during the recital of her licentious past, that she was the daughter of a pope.

At times the full force of the satire was driven home quite succinctly. For example, the pride of the Spanish was satirized by the use of a name, given without comment: Don Fernando d'Ibaraa y Figueora y Mascarenes y Lampourdos y Souza. The excessive pride of the Germans, on the other hand, is pricked by numerous references to Cunégonde's seventy-two quarters, which placed her hopelessly beyond Candide's social level. The Eldorado episode is derogatory toward court flattery at the French court and human greed in general, among other things. In his dealings with the shipowners, Candide was thoroughly fleeced; even more avaricious, however, were the publishers, against whom Voltaire carried on a personal vendetta, having suffered so often at their hands. Judges and doctors are, naturally, lampooned. When Candide fell ill in Paris, the doctors flocked to his bedside, having learned that he was rich. Martin commented "I remember having been ill in Paris during my first trip; I was very poor, therefore, I had neither friends, religious attendants, nor doctors, and I got cured" [XXI:188]. The charlatanry or simple ineptitude of doctors never escaped Voltaire's barbs, and eighteenth-century medicine offered him a wealth of material for such observations as: "However, by means of medicines and bleedings, the illness of Candide became serious" [XXI:188]. Throughout his life, Voltaire despised gambling, all the more so because Emilie had been such a devotee of it. Drawing on personal experience, Voltaire related in *Candide* that our hero was cheated out of 50,000 francs, "after which they dined gaily."

Women and romantic love are recurrent targets in *Candide* of Voltaire's derision and cynicism, just as they were in *Zadig* and his other works. All the women in *Candide* are pictured as selfish, cheap, heartless, and sometimes just vicious. The old woman and Paquette are the worst specimens, but Cunégonde was quite willing to abandon Candide, her devoted lover, because the Spanish grandee was richer and more powerful! To reach this momentous decision, Cunégonde required only "a quarter of an hour" [XXI:163]. At a supper in Paris, during which the conversation was typically banal, insipid, and slanderous, a young marquise noticed the two large diamonds on Candide's fingers. She "praised them so earnestly, that they passed from his fingers to those of the marquise" [XII:193]. And there is the farcical scene in which an abbé employed a young woman to impersonate a sick Cunégonde in order to extort more diamonds from Candide. Instead of arresting the abbé or the young woman, the police seized Martin and Candide, who, fearing the uncertainties of legal procedure, preferred to bribe the officials to insure their liberty. A visit to Pococurante, a Venetian gentleman most appropriately named, offered Voltaire the opportunity to satirize the chicanery and hypocrisy in music, art, and literature. Pococurante, whom Voltaire claimed to resemble, was a cynic, bored with everything. Yet many of his judgments are still sound and valid today.

The main attack centers on the philosophy of optimism, primarily through the character Pangloss, who symbolizes vain speculation and metaphysical pretensions. Voltaire presents him as a teacher of "métaphysico-théologo-cosmolo-nigologie." The sheer futility of argument over things beyond the ken of man is demonstrated by a fruitless discussion between Candide, the faithful disciple of Pangloss, and the more realistic Martin. "They debated for a full two weeks on end, and at the end of that time, they were as advanced as on the first day" [XXI:185]. Sometimes the object of Voltaire's satire is multiple, as in the following sentence, wherein Rousseau, optimism, and the Jesuits are simultaneously subjected to ridicule: "After all, the state of pure nature must be good, since these people, instead of eating me, showed me a thousand kindnesses once they knew I was not a Jesuit" [XXI:172]. (This is Candide's exclamation, after having been spared by the Oreillon savages.) Faulty logic was on occasion deliberately used with telling effect, as in Pangloss' rebuttal to Jacques' recital of evil and misery: "'All that is indispensable,' replied the one-eyed doctor; 'individual misfortunes account for the general good; so that the more individual misfortunes there are, the better everything in general is' " [XXI:146]. The irony behind this defense of optimism lies in the fact that Pangloss has just lost an eye and an ear as a result of the syphilis Paquette had given him. And as Pangloss sang the praises of benevolent Providence, "the air darkened, the winds blew hard from all directions, and the ship was engulfed by a horrible tempest, within sight of the port of Lisbon" [XXI:146]—the site, significantly, of the disastrous earthquake that had actually taken over 30,000 lives and wreaked incalculable property damage. In Voltaire's earthquake, all the passengers on the ship drown except Candide, Pangloss (the tale must go on after all), and the scoundrel who had drowned the virtuous Anabaptist Jacques. The preservation of the last of these three is an insidious Voltairean stroke to underscore the type of justice practiced by Providence.

Is it any wonder, when the scope and passionate strength of *Candide* are taken into account, that Anatole France was able to refer to *Candide* and *Don Quixote* as two "manuals of pity and indulgence, bibles of goodwill"? [11] Such is the blindness of prejudice, however, that, in the face of this monumental evidence of Voltaire's humanitarianism, he has actually been compared by a later commentator to a vulture living by and on the ruins he created around him.

L'INGENU

The last tale to be examined is *L'Ingénu*, a satire of social and political hypocrisy, too long neglected in favor of *Candide*, *Zadig*, and *Micromégas*, in spite of Voltaire's preference for this work. Grimm, who had been unable to appreciate the value of *Candide*, expressed amazement over *L'Ingénu*: "It is a unique phenomenon that a man 74 years old can write with so much gaiety, grace, and fire—with such charm and prodigious facility." [12] More significant, because the praise comes from someone normally less favorably disposed toward Voltaire than Grimm, was the criticism of

Louis-Mayeul Chaudon: "there is more sprightliness and easy flow, more subtlety and grace in *L'Ingénu* than in *Candide*. . . . It has numerous passages which sparkle with brightness of style and grace of expression." [13]

The plot-line of *L'Ingénu* differs from the other *contes* because of its greater credibility, and the historical verisimilitude of the setting, more faithfully adhered to, creates an added interest for the reader. For the most part, it is devoid of the surface mockery of human weaknesses to be found in *Zadig* and *Candide,* the exaggerated presentation of which tends to disguise the deadly seriousness behind the persiflage and burlesque. Moreover the characters of *L'Ingénu* are more lifelike. The reader can more easily identify with them, can become more involved in their fate than is possible with the puppet characters of the other tales. This is especially true of Mlle. St.-Yves and the Huron, particularly in the third and final section of the story, where Mlle. St.-Yves heroically liberates her lover at the cost of her honor and tragically dies, having decided in her innocence that love and marriage cannot survive her betrayal. Cynically, but with great psychological insight, Voltaire commented: "She did not realize how virtuous she had been in committing the crime for which she reproached herself" [XXI:293].

Great changes in the characters are necessarily effected too quickly in so short a "novel," and therefore some improbability was inescapable. But the reader-character identification remains in *L'Ingénu* to a degree that was impossible in *Candide,* despite the latter's greater unity, fashioned as it was by a central theme—the attack on philosophical optimism—and the constant tension maintained between the pessimism of the facts and the optimism of the presentation. *L'Ingénu* lacks the rapidly-moving account of adventures of *Zadig* and *Candide;* it moves more slowly, and the incidents are less numerous, thus giving the reader ample time to immerse himself in the thoughts and actions of the characters.

In some respects *L'Ingénu* represents a more severe indictment of the weeds in the human garden than is put forward by the other tales, precisely because of its concern for the dignity and liberty of man. No work of Voltaire highlights so vividly the terrible injustice of being thrown into prison without trial. For J. H. Brumfitt, "the real central theme of *L'Ingénu* is not philosophical but political" [14]; Daniel Mornet likewise construed the work as a satire of the administrative workings of the Ancien Régime.[15] The hero himself presents a striking example of political injustice: he is summarily thrown into the Bastille on the unsupported accusations of his enemies. Gordon, his Jansenist cell-mate, has suffered the same fate at the hands of his Jesuit adversary, Father La Chaise, who, finding the Jansenist's views on the role of the pope intolerable, "obtained from the king, his penitent, an order to deprive him, without formality of justice, of the most precious gift man possesses, his liberty" [XXI:273].

In 1761, just a few years before the publication of *L'Ingénu,* the inextricable mixture of religion and politics in the eighteenth century which, dramatized by the struggles between the Jesuits and Jansenists, became public when the Jesuit Father La Valette, who had encountered financial difficulties in his commercial enterprises in Martinique, mistakenly appealed his case to the Jansenist controlled Parliament. The ensuing furor enabled the Jansenists to seek their revenge for the reversals they had suffered at the hands of the Jesuits during the early years of the century as a result of the two Jesuit inspired papal Bulls: *Vineam Domini* of 1705 and *Unigenitus* of 1713. Because of Father La Valette's tactical blunder, the Jansenists succeeded in condemning the work of the Jesuits in 1761, depriving them of the control of the colleges; in the following year, they managed to suppress the order altogether. So acrimonious had the feud become that the populace openly resented the intrusion of religion into politics and commerce. The involvement of the clergy in the latter had been pronounced enough to compel Pope Benedict XIV in 1741 to interdict commercial undertakings, especially in slave traffic.

Whatever differences exist between *L'Ingénu* and the other philosophical tales, it still contains many of the satirical thrusts common to the body of Voltaire's work. He starts the tale with an attack upon the Church by referring to Saint Dunstan as "Irish by birth and a Saint by profession" [XXI.247]. The goodness of Abbé Kerkabon, stressed throughout the narrative, serves as a contrast for the incontinence and immorality of the other ecclesiasts. Voltaire firmly believed that priests should lead normal lives, in conformance with the physiological oneness of man. He bristled at the hypocritical behavior of priests who were supposed to be setting ethical standards for their flocks. Repetitively, even *ad nauseam,* Voltaire depicted churchmen as lascivious, gluttonous, and fanatical. In *L'Ingénu* the visits Abbé Kerkabon and his sister paid to three bishops were unsuccessful because each bishop was too busy entertaining a lady friend, who was closeted with him in order to discuss Church matters.

The liberal recourse to dispensations was condemned several times, and in this connection the pope himself was not spared. Indeed, as the head of Catholicism—the religion naturally best known to Voltaire, and therefore held most responsible for the physical and mental ills of mankind—the pope was the symbol of evil. " 'All the unfortunate persons I have met,' " the Huron concluded after a discussion with the Jansenist Gordon, " 'are so because of the pope' " [XXI:273]. The nefarious influence of popes was for Voltaire a matter of history. In the *Essai sur les moeurs,* Voltaire delivers himself of several biting tirades against popes.

> Throughout many centuries popes were armed when elected; and the people, even the princes, were such imbeciles that a person known to them as an anti-pope, once elected, was from that moment the Vicar of God and an infallible man. When that infallible man was deposed, one revered the Divinity in his successor; and these Gods on earth, sometimes assassins, sometimes assassinated, poisoners and poisoned in turn, enriching their bastards and handing down decrees against fornication, anathematizing tourneys while waging wars, excommunicating and deposing kings, and selling dispensations of sins to one and all, were at one and the same time the scandal, the horror, and the divinity of Catholic Europe [XIII:176].

The irresponsible behavior of some popes did not, however, prevent Voltaire from recognizing the good performed by others. For example, he singled out Pope Alexander III for his meritorious actions: his attempt to abolish slavery in the twelfth century, his diplomatic handling of the unreasonable emperor Frederick Barbarossa, and his pressure on Henry II of England to demand pardon of God and man for having had Thomas Becket murdered.

Ordinarily Voltaire was interested in exposing the weaknesses of the Church. He delighted in describing the interview between Mlle. St.-Yves and the Jesuit confessor, Father Tout-à-tous, to whom she had gone for advice on how to answer St. Pouange's demand that she submit physically to him in return for the freedom of her lover. The Jesuitical casuistry employed to justify her submission, once he had learned that the seducer was the powerful St. Pouange, is delightful. First he counseled her not to use the word lover, for that could offend God. Husband was more appropriate, even though they were not actually married. Second, she could not be guilty of adultery, since in fact she was not yet married. Third, when the intention was pure, the action could not be bad; and finally, he assured her, the Scriptures offered many examples to justify her conduct. After which he added hypocritically: "Mind you, I am not advising you, but you are wise, and one can hope that you will be useful to your husband. Monsignor de St. Pouange is an honest man; he will not betray you" [XXI:289].

The conversion and baptism of the Huron, which became possible once they recognized that he had been blessed with Grace, offered fruitful opportunities for satire. In describing the confession that preceded the baptism, Voltaire seized every opening to question the Church dogmas that had no basis in the Scriptures. In a burlesque scene, the Huron, following to the letter the Scriptural injunction, "Confess your sins one to the other," forced his confessor in turn to kneel and confess. The joy of baptizing "a Lower Breton English Huron" was so great, Voltaire said, that the singular event was overlooked. The Huron's remonstrance to the baptism itself on the grounds that "in England one was allowed to live as he chose" [XXI:252] went unheeded. Needless to say, no discussion of the evil implicit in religion ever omitted the reliance by fanatics upon Providence. Everyone admired the mysterious ways of Providence that had caused the Huron to turn up in their midst. And the discovery, made upon the flimsiest of evidence, that he was the nephew of the Kerkabons only increased their admiration before the workings of Providence. Indeed Chapters 5 and 6, in spite of their narrative simplicity, represent as virulent a diatribe against the customs and practices of the Church as can be found in Voltaire, all the more effective because the characters seem to be made of flesh and blood. Thus Mlle. St.-Yves' confinement in a convent to keep her from her lover is as dramatic an exposure as it is of the practice of forcing unwilling souls into a religious life, because she has become a real person to the reader.

Throughout the "novel" as a whole, Voltaire sets Natural Law, the best guide for man, against the arbitrary rules and customs that run counter to the normal instincts and desires of social beings. It is ironic that, in presenting the contrast between savage and civilized man in this work, Voltaire seemingly adopts the fundamental philosophy of his archenemy, Jean-Jacques Rousseau, from whom he had become completely estranged by the time he wrote *L'Ingénu*. The marked difference in their positions, which separates them unalterably despite their superficial rapprochement, is shown by Voltaire in his contrast of the Natural Law of the savage with the structured institutions of society, in order to demonstrate the injustice and inhumanity produced by arbitrarily and excessively contrived organisms such as the Church. Moreover, he is definitely trying to extract the maximum possible humor from this juxtaposition. Neither the savage nor society is completely right or wrong. Once again the philosophy of Babouc prevails—namely, that there is good and bad in both; only in this case the bad in the savage is simply ludicrous, whereas that which is found in society is injurious. The following incident corroborates the moderation advocated by Voltaire. The Huron, pursuing the dictates of his heart and relying upon the moral code supposedly observed by the savages, boldly entered Mlle. St.-Yves' bedroom and would in all good conscience have possessed her. The virtuous young woman, in spite of her sincere love and desire for him, was restrained by her social upbringing and religious precepts; she cried out in alarm. Her brother, the abbé, and the governess rushed in;

they told the Ingénu that society did not permit such forth-right behavior. The Huron tried to defend his actions on the basis of Natural Law, and momentarily the abbé found it difficult to convince the young savage. But eventually the abbé's reasoning impresses the Huron, who has a good and upright mind. The fact that the latter accepts the rationality of his remarks proves that Voltaire supported the organizations of socialized man, so long as they did not violate the eternal and infrangible rights of man implicit in Natural Law.

The Huron's prison experiences offer additional evidence of Voltaire's continuing identity with all the civilizing forces, as opposed to Rousseau's position. The role that books played in the life of the Huron during his incarceration amply demonstrates Voltaire's preference for the life of culture and progress, in which books are a consolation and edification. The Huron's naive soul has been so transformed by his exposure to literature that he is driven to exclaim: "I'm tempted to believe in metamorphoses, for I have been changed from a brute to a man'" [XXI:276]. Final proof can be found in the Huron's selection of Europe over Canada precisely because the civilizing effect of the arts and sciences has improved the natural state of man over what he remembered it to have been in Canada. The scales could not be tipped too much in favor of civilization, to be sure, in view of the many ills wrought by organizations within society. To counterbalance his obvious predilection for progress, therefore, Voltaire has the Jansenist Gordon exclaim:

"What! I have spent fifty years instructing myself, and I fear I can not match the good natural common sense of this child who is almost a savage! I tremble when I realize how laboriously I have fortified my prejudices; whereas he listens only to simple nature" [XXI:278].

Inasmuch as it is a Jansenist who speaks these words, this clearly is not intended to be an unqualified paean of praise for simple nature and common sense unfortified by learning. The most one can say unequivocally is that the Huron's simplicity is preferable to the prejudiced views of fanatics.

Any extended work of Voltaire invariably includes satire against the medical profession. *L'Ingénu* is no exception. When Mlle. St.-Yves falls ill from remorse, the contribution of the two doctors is as ineffective as that of the doctors in *Zadig* and *Candide*. All the doctors manage to do is to worsen the patient's condition.

> [The first doctor] was one of those who visits his patients on the run, confusing the illness he has just treated with that of the patient before him. . . . He made her illness twice as dangerous by his haste to prescribe a remedy then in fashion. There was fashion even in medicine. This folly was too common in Paris [XXI:299].

After the first doctor's failure to make any noticeable improvement, a second doctor was called. Thanks to his ministrations, "the illness became fatal in two days" [XXI:299].

Another pet grievance of Voltaire was the incessant social chatter at the dinner table, objectionable to him, no doubt, because the garrulity of dinner guests must at times have prevented the irrepressible Voltaire from dominating the conversation. The provincialism of the French was also scored by Voltaire, whose interest in humanity easily transcended the mental restrictions and limitations represented by national boundaries. To the Huron's assertion that his language was the most beautiful, Mlle. Kerkabon replied: " 'Is it possible? I thought that French was the most beautiful of all the languages after Low Breton' " [XXI:250]. Voltaire's insistence upon giving his views on every conceivable subject often, in fact, marred his work. In *L'Ingénu* the section on the theater is nothing more than a gratuitous insertion of the author's personal opinions; it destroys the unity of the work. On the whole, however, this *conte* comes closer to qualifying as a "short novel" than does any of his other works. Perhaps it was Voltaire's interest in maintaining a greater semblance of the novel form that caused him to deviate from his anti-feminist pattern and present the portrait of a sympathetic heroine. From another point of view, this work—like all of Volaire's writings, whatever the genre— falls into the well-known formula that is identifiable with the practical moralist and realist. The sharp contrast set up between the well-thinking and well-intentioned Huron and the courtiers at Versailles, who thought only in terms of self-aggrandizement and self-interest, underlines the usual Voltairean message so eloquently summarized by the Huron, when he explains to the nonplussed Versailles official, "'In a word, I wish to be useful'" [XXI:270].

The content of the philosophical tales gives evidence of the moral philosopher in every paragraph. Voltaire is unabashedly didactic and polemical. Content alone cannot, of course, create a masterpiece, no matter how universal the ideas or how broad the canvas. But "if Voltaire is a moralist of genius," Henry Brailsford informs us, "he is also an extraordinarily gifted prose artist. Indeed he is frequently both at the same time in a very special combination, and nowhere more effectively than in *Candide*.[16] And George Havens ventures the opinion that Voltaire's dominant influence in modern times is perhaps upon style. Yet so crammed are his works with ideas, so iterative is the stroke of the polemicist, that many critics are reluctant to rank Voltaire among writers of the first magnitude. One would almost gather that ideas have become suspect in literature. Voltaire did repeat himself, to be sure; he was, after all, fighting the same enemies at every turn. Yet the humanism of Voltaire included, as humanism should, a passionate obsession with language, an almost sensual love of words that elevated writing above the simple act of communication. The expression of the thought was still paramount, but the command of language enabled the writer to express those thoughts in all the nuances that are conceivable to a cultured and refined mind.

The best defense of Voltaire's stature as a writer rests precisely on the quality judged indispensable by contemporary critics—that is, style. In truth, no one, Flaubert not excepted, possessed a more unerring instinct and infallible genius for selecting the correct word or the best turn of phrase. The superlative results Flaubert achieved in *Madame Bovary* through laborious effort, Voltaire seemingly produced spontaneously—though only seemingly for, as he admitted himself, he reworked everything even after publication. So ingrained was this habit that he once asserted that there would never be a final edition of any of his works during his lifetime. Voltaire's verbal gift was aided by an exceptional aural sensitivity. Add to these his universally acknowledged sparkling wit and trenchant satire, and all the tools were at hand to present his ideas in their sharpest possible focus. The efficacy of his style, then, lay in his ability to make the felicitous choice of word or phrase so as to render succinctly the desired effect. No description of Voltaire's style is more apt than the comparison with "a translucent stream of purest mountain water, moving with swift and animated flow under flashing sunbeams." [17]

Because of Voltaire's facility, there has been much speculation as to the length of time it took him to write *Candide*. The latest criticism tends to discount the previously held theory, based principally on Wagnière's testimony, that he dashed off this "bagatelle" in three days or three weeks. That he wrote it rapidly no one doubts; he was after all at the peak of his intellectual powers, recent events had fired his emotions to white heat, and he had an almost limitless fount of material available to him from the tremendous research entailed by his historical writings. The re-examination of this problem by critics like René Pomeau and William Bottiglia, following the recent discovery of the La Vallière manuscript by Ira Wade, has established the likelihood that Voltaire started the work early in 1758 and returned to it intermittently throughout the year. Whatever the truth may be, with Voltaire there is little need to correlate length of time and quality of work. By everyone's admission he was peculiarly endowed with all the intellectual qualities and writing skills that are necessary to write beautifully, without the necessity for those tedious revisions that are normally unavoidable for the less gifted writer. Theodore Besterman asserts:

> One thing is certain; Voltaire will emerge as a carefully painstaking writer—not merely a generalizer of genius, careless about detail; as a man of considerable and accurate verbal memory in several languages; in general, as a man whose universal interests were not merely the play of a restless, inquisitive mind but were based on wide reading and inquiry, recorded day by day throughout a long life.[18]

One of the most characteristic qualities of Voltaire's prose is its vivacity, achieved in large part by the frequent use of

short sentences and the elimination of conjunctives. The
punch effect is sometimes delivered by an artistic reliance
on the past definite tense. *Zadig* offers the most frequent
use of this stylistic device, both single verbs for surprise or
satire, and successions of verbs to create the sensation of
rapid action. Translation unfortunately destroys the full
impact of this tense, so in the few examples given the
French will be given before the English.

A ces paroles, il se jeta à ses genoux et les baigna de
larmes. Astarté le releva tendrement, et elle continua ainsi
[XXI:81].

*At these words, he threw himself at her feet and bathed
them with his tears. Astarté tenderly raised him and she
continued thus.*

Zadig eut la curiosité de voir ce que cette femme écrivait;
il s'approcha, il vit la lettre Z, puis un A; il fut étonné;
puis parut un D; il tressaillit [XXI:77–78].

*Zadig had a curiosity to see what the woman was writing;
he approached, saw the letter Z, then an A; he was
amazed; then appeared a D; he trembled.*

The remainder of the incident continues at the same rapid
pace. *L'Ingénu,* though less swift-moving, offers some excellent examples of this "punch" delivery. When the Abbé
Kerkabon and his sister asked the bishop to help them lo-
cate their nephew, the Jesuit replied he would do everything in his power to help, then: "Il congédia affectueuse-
ment le prieur, et n'y pensa plus" [XXI:282]. ("He
warmly dismissed the prior and didn't give it another
thought.")

In analyzing the rhythm of Voltaire's prose, Gustave
Lanson claims that Voltaire stripped his sentences down to
the essential action words, thereby giving his prose a bedev-
iled movement that carries the reader along at a tremendous pace.[19] Periodically, in order to achieve greater impact
through contrast, Voltaire deliberately altered the pace by
inserting co-ordinating words and subordinate clauses to
parody the periodic eloquence of the interminable pastoral
novels still popular in the eighteenth century. Notable exam-

ples are Chapters 8 and 11 in *Candide,* respectively the history of Cunégonde's adventures before her reunion with Candide, and the longer history of the old woman's misfortunes and escapades. Significantly, the latter are told at more than twice the length, since Voltaire could permit himself greater license with the old woman than with the heroine. Unforgettable too are the delightful lines one unexpectedly encounters, like Mlle. St.-Yves' pathetic retort to St. Poulange's demand that she yield to his advances: "'Ah! how I would love you, if only you did not want to be loved so much!'" [XXI:291].

Conciseness and compression are likewise employed, more frequently in *Candide* than in *Zadig* or the other tales, to attain the fast pace of Voltairean prose. This is accomplished by telescoping the narrative or dialogue, giving cumulative catalogues and enumerative summaries, or through the use of flashback meditations. William Bottiglia found at least seventy examples in *Candide* alone.[20]

Often, according to Ruth Flowers, the exposure of a vice will depend on "a word, wittily placed and ironically stressed, so as to surprise the reader, or strike him, or trick him into consciousness of the evil being criticized or denounced."[21] Sometimes repetition produces the devastating results desired, and when it is skillfully combined with alliteration, the stylistic effect is so intriguing that any attempt to translate would be doomed to failure: "Je connus la canaille écrivante, la canaille cabalante, et la canaille convulsionnaire" [XXI:186]. The poet's reliance on the sound of words is evident in everything he wrote. Consequently, examples of onomatopoeia appear frequently. André Le Breton emphasizes Voltaire's gift "for finding names, the sounds of which are in themselves a joy to the reader."[22] A review of the names of the characters in *Candide* is convincing proof that Voltaire must have had their sound value as well as their suggestive meanings in mind when he selected them: Candide, Cunégonde, Cacambo, Pangloss, Paquette, Pococurante, not to mention the elaborate names already alluded to, which were designed to satirize empty pride. The aural effect is not only prominent but subtle, in the judgment of Henry Brailsford, who rather generously compares *Candide* to "a quartette of Mozart's: so light it seems, so graceful, so easy, that one supposes that none of its beauties can escape an attentive ear at the first playing, yet every repetition is discovery." [23]

The irony, burlesque, and satire of Voltaire are often rendered by understatements, contrasts, or the union of absurdities. Memorable are such statements as "Pangloss lost *only* one eye and one ear" during the cure; Candide after three weeks of medication "already had a little skin and could walk"; or ironic contradictions like "boucherie héroïque" and "un bel auto-da-fé." In retrospect, the reader finds that the most terrible things have evoked a smile. Who can resist such a smile when Candide, horribly tortured by the Bulgares, pleads to be killed to end his suffering, and "he obtained this favor" [XXI:141]. But the master polemicist knew what he was doing. This disciple of Molière was all too aware that reflection invariably accompanies or follows the laughter provoked by extravagant and ludicrous episodes. Though the work of Voltaire is replete with satire, which is unquestionably his trade mark and his favorite weapon, he was capable of delightful irony on occasion. An example in *Candide* is the following comment by Martin: "The Doge has his troubles, the gondoliers have theirs. It is true that all considered the fate of the gondolier is preferable to that of the Doge, but I find the difference so negligible that it is not worth the trouble to point it out" [XXI:201]. Similar jabs appear with great frequency throughout the works of Voltaire. The 1739 variant of "Sur les Pensées de Pascal," contained these words: "I seek only the truth; I think it is quite correct that the Christian religion should not be proved by metaphysics, and that reason is as inferior to faith as the finite is to the infinite. My remarks deal only with reason, and it is so relatively unimportant among men that it is not worth getting excited over this." [24]

In fact, contrary to recent critics who refuse to see irony in the rich symbolical connotations of the garden figure, we find the whole of *Candide*, especially the conclusion, a masterpiece of irony. Throughout *Candide* we have our hero's refrain that all is well, as Pangloss has repeatedly insisted, or at least that all will be well in spite of present ills, once he has managed to find Cunégonde. The reality at the end of the long quest reduces all his dreams and convictions to ashes. Certainly no one can realistically argue that the social meliorism promised by the garden figure eliminates the disappointment that Candide, the man and lover, must have experienced. And one of the finest forms of irony is a turn of events, the opposite of what one could logically have anticipated.

The richness of Voltaire's style stems from the varied arsenal that he drew upon so effectively in his campaign to bring about reforms through ridicule. In the process he created a style typically Voltairean, proven by the ease with which his contemporaries could generally recognize his work, in spite of his repeated denials of authorship in order to avoid persecution. The same month that *L'Ingénu* appeared, August 1767, one critic wrote:

> There is much discussion about a new novel entitled *L'Ingénu*. It has more than 200 pages and piques one's curiosity all the more since it is difficult to obtain and is obviously the work of a writer who is customarily much in demand. People compare it with *Candide;* it is from the same author. It would be difficult for him to retain his anonymity; he has a style and characteristic wit which easily betray him.[25]

Paradoxically, the style accepted as Voltairean is different from the eloquence and sonority of the classical writings, although he remained the outstanding spokesman of classicism. The identifying qualities of Voltaire's *style coupé* are: brevity, facility of expression, irony, wit, satire, burlesque, parody, and above all clarity (notwithstanding the allegorical and symbolical aspects some critics have attributed to his work).

Voltaire, the inimitable prose stylist, "for whom the resources, nuances, and delicacy of the French language held no secrets," [26] may have lacked the warmth and enthusiasm of Rousseau, the picturesqueness and color of Diderot, and the naivete and passion of Prévost, but he also avoided the inaccuracies of Diderot, the often misplaced grandiloquence of Rousseau, and the platitudes of Prévost. Yet critics continue to underrate Voltaire. They find him the victim of his facile form and brilliant wit—a failure whenever he attempted any serious and protracted literary work. They also deny him the soul and imagination of the poet and find him "grounded" at the mundane level of things, unwilling or unable to strive for the ideal world of the truly creative literary mind. Despite this all too common disparagement of Voltaire's literary achievements, he unquestionably possessed the verbal skills of a poet and to these skills he brought a sense of humor that was nourished by cynicism but rooted in humanity. He employed a cutting satire and irony that drew its power from as sharp a wit and intelligence as the world has ever seen. The result has been devastating to his enemies, beneficial and entertaining to his friends, and a delight for readers of all time.

CHAPTER III

THE HISTORICAL WORKS

OF VOLTAIRE

At the time Voltaire started to write his *contes*, his reputation as an historian, today his second strongest claim to immortality, still lay ahead of him. He had published only the *Histoire de Charles XII*, the dramatic and narrative qualities of which had led readers and critics alike into misjudging its merits as history. It was a logical error, for this successor to Racine had instinctively selected a hero who was great enough to merit historical treatment, unfortunate enough to inspire the dramatist, and mad enough to serve as grist for the never-ceasing mills of polemic, ever primary in the mind of Voltaire. Because history, in his opinion, should edify man, Voltaire was for many years convinced that a knowledge of recent events was bound to be more profitable to the reader than that of the long distant past. In his *Conseils à un journaliste (Advice to a Journalist)* he gave this advice: "Inspire the young to develop a taste for the history of modern times that is useful to us instead of ancient history, which serves only to satisfy our curiosity" [XII:244].

In selecting Charles XII as the subject of his first major history, Voltaire thus followed his own counsel; the dramatist in him made the most of his material, as he sought deliberately to arouse the curiosity of his readers. What he disliked about the historians Mézeray and Daniel, he confessed in a letter to d'Argenson, was their inability to interest him: "They bore me, because they can neither paint nor stir one's passions" [Best. 2030]. Twelve years later, in a letter to President Hénault, author of the beneficial and therefore laudable *Abrégé de l'Histoire de la France* (*Concise History of France*), he elaborated on his method of writing history:

> My goal was to inject interest into historical facts rendered boring by all who had treated them before me. . . . My secret is to force the reader to ask himself: Will Philippe V be king? Will Holland be destroyed? Will Louis XIV succumb? In a word, I wish to arouse the emotions of readers of history [Best. 4163].

One can readily see why Voltaire's *Charles XII* presented a striking contrast with the boring six-volume work of Limiers and the prejudiced biography by Nordberg, the former confessor of Charles XII.

Before Voltaire appeared on the scene to make of history a science, just as Montesquieu had done with politics, historical studies were not only uninteresting but also unreliable. With the exception of Thucydides and Xenophon, the Greek and Roman historians had, in Voltaire's opinion, filled their works with boring fables, which necessitated the suspension of one's reasoning powers. What gave Voltaire grave cause for concern was the incredible fact that the same degree of credulity existed in his own day, in a nation supposedly enlightened by the presence and activity of many *philosophes*. This realization led to his decision systematically and ruthlessly to separate history from myth. The history of early centuries especially contained absurdities in abundance, both conscious and unconscious. An example of the latter type was the story of Queen Brunehilde, still faithfully reported in such better histories as Hénault's *Nouvel Abrégé* (*New Summary*) of 1744. According to the generally accepted legend, the God-fearing and humane king had the Queen put to death in a savage and inhumane manner. First she was tied by her hair and leg to the tail of a wild horse; then she was dragged to her death. Voltaire found that the tale violated reason; he questioned among other things the veracity of a report in which an eighty-year-old woman was tied to a horse's tail by her sparse hair and a leg. Even worse were what Voltaire felt to be the deliberate falsehoods of those who pretended to speak in the name of God, for they thereby blasphemed against God and betrayed their fellowmen.

The vast majority of the early historical works, especially the multi-volumed *Annales* of pre-Christian and early Christian times, were primarily chronologies, which displayed geographical rather than historical completeness. The studies of the religiously oriented historians of succeeding centuries were in some ways even less reliable, because of their heavy dependence upon a providential interpretation of events. The outstanding representative of the latter group was Bossuet who, in Voltaire's estimation, presented religious distortions of history with elegance and force. Despite his undeniable style and eloquence, the "illustrious Bossuet" explained ancient history on the basis of a literal interpretation of the Bible; he saw human destiny as controlled by the interference of Providence. His religious bias made Mohammedans sound like a horde of barbarians. Nonetheless, in the *Discours sur l'histoire universelle* (*Discourse on Universal History*, 1681) Bossuet did foreshadow and defend the universal approach to history.[1]

Probably the most common type of history during the seventeenth century and the first part of the eighteenth was the work of the so-called humanist historians, who wrote historical novels rather than histories. So blurred had the line become between novel and history, that Courtilz de Sandras, the author of *Mémoires de d'Artagnan* (*Memoirs of d'Artagnan,* 1700), could be mistakenly included in the list of historians. Unfortunately, what the humanist historians produced were political biographies filled with recitals of court pageantry, military feats and diplomatic intrigues. Voltaire attacked "their credulity and lack of critical sense, their national and religious prejudices, their insignificant and useless details, their preoccupation with battles and genealogies, and their falsifications and defamations. He was equally critical of their harangues, portraits, and other outmoded rhetorical devices."[2] Voltaire believed in a philosophical or intellectual history, an analytical rather than a chronological, geographical, or biographical approach. He was, in short, an historian for whom the fact remained the cornerstone of history, because "a true fact was worth more than a hundred antitheses" [XV:124]. Dramatist though he himself was, he strenuously opposed, for that reason, the tendency of the seventeenth-century historians Vertot and Saint-Réal to alter facts with the freedom of dramatists.

The historian had to be faithful to the filiated facts, not to the non-filiated ones that had little bearing on the course of history. Events, episodes, and anecdotes, which were interesting only as gossip or to illuminate the eccentricities and foibles of kings, contributed little to a knowledge of the over-all progress of the human mind and society. Voltaire shifted the emphasis from the character and life of an individual to the character and spirit of peoples. The chronologies of kings could serve as guideposts, but not as goals, for the historian should always think in the broad terms of peoples rather than of individual men. The only princes worthy of personal histories in any case, Voltaire insisted, were those "who had done some good for humanity" [XVI:130]. The role of the historian was different from that of the journalist, who was concerned with trivia of passing interest. This explains why Voltaire chided Nordberg's concentration on insignificant details—such as the color and size of chairs, the precise hour that Charles XII performed inconsequential acts—while completely overlooking the state of Sweden's economy and military strength—why Charles XII was crowned before the age prescribed by law, and why the queen mother was deprived of her regency.

The insufficient research of most historians particularly exasperated Voltaire. The distortion of unimportant details, something the most conscientious researcher might commit, could be of minor significance, a mere isolated erratum. On the other hand, when historical blunders distorted conclusions regarding the customs, legislation, and civilization of a nation, then the harm was incalculable. The works of Joinville, Mézeray, Daniel, Pufendorf, and Nordberg too often were marred by inaccuracies of this kind.

My *Histoire de Charles XII* is not written in this vein. I can assure you that if ever a history merited the credence of the reader, it is this one [XVI:128].

He prided himself on scrupulous impartiality and careful research:

> I had no *parti-pris;* truth was my sole object; not that truth
> for details that characterize nothing, teach nothing, and
> are therefore worthless; but the truth that develops the
> genius of the ruler, the court, and the nation. The work
> could have been much better, but it could not have had a
> more noble goal [XV:141].

In seeking materials for his *Siècle de Louis XIV,* Voltaire proclaimed his intent to write history not as a flatterer, a panegyrist, or a gazetteer, but as a philosopher.

The progression noticeable in the three historical works to be discussed: *Histoire de Charles XII* (1731), *Siècle de Louis XIV* (1751), and *Essai sur les moeurs* (1756), attest to the realization of Voltaire's ambition and his right to the title of "Historian of Humanity." From the individual, Charles XII, he broadened his view in the *Siècle* to include an epoch, and in the *Essai* he finally abandoned the Europocentric conception of history to embrace the universal. Whatever the debt may have been that Voltaire owed to Bolingbroke, he did adopt Bolingbroke's dictum: "History is philosophy teaching by examples," as he attempted to interpret the past in terms that were applicable to his own time. This remained essentially the guiding principle of all his works, even when he gradually abandoned Bolingbroke's theory that the distant past could be less immediately useful than a knowledge of recent events.

A giant step toward the realization of philosophical or intellectual history was Voltaire's transfer of the direction of events from a mystical, incomprehensible Providence onto the shoulders of man, by the adoption of the principle of natural causation. In doing so, he opened the way for a more rigorously scientific investigation of the laws of progress. The inability to adhere consistently, however, to "anything resembling a unified conception of causation," [3] resulted from the importance that Voltaire attached to the role of chance, in spite of the fact that his belief in a universe built on orderly lines necessitated the embodiment of cause and effect in human history. Many major occurrences, he was fond of saying, had been determined by the smallest of incidents. A favorite example, based on a story originally told by Bolingbroke, was the story of the glass of water the Duchess of Marlborough, who had been rendered clumsy by jealousy, inadvertently spilled on Queen Anne—thereby "changing the face of Europe." Another was the simple mistake of the messenger who went to Augerville instead of Angerville, as a result of which Condé received the message too late to prevent France from remaining bogged down in civil war.

Needless to say, the total impartiality proclaimed by Voltaire was impossible of attainment, least of all by Voltaire himself, and he would probably have had to resort to major surgery to rid himself of the eighteenth-century fondness for anecdotes. But his intentions were excellent, and on the whole he succeeded to a degree unmatched by any historian before or during his time. By example and precept, he managed to discredit such previously sacrosanct historians as Livy, Tacitus, Plutarch, Suetonius, and Herodotus. The Renaissance fared better: he admired Machiavelli's *Discours sur la première Décade de Tite-Live* (*Discourses on Livy,* begun before *The Prince* of 1513 but finished later), Guicciardini's *Histoire d'Italie* (*History of Italy,* 1561–1564), and De Thou's *Histoire de mon temps* (*History of My Time,* 1604). These writers represented for him the fathers of modern history. The seventeenth century, by contrast, had produced little work of value. Even François Eude de Mézeray and Gabriel Daniel, who were generally considered to be the best historians of their times, had emphasized incidents as against ideas and filled their works with inaccuracies. Mézeray, historiographer of France, had in his *Histoire de France* (1643–1651) confused history with kings. The work for the most part was a gallery of portraits of kings and queens, accompanied by a brief résumé of each life—boring trivia, meaningless as history, and filled with mistakes. Daniel, the Jesuit historiographer of France and author of chronological summaries of Louis XIII and Louis XIV, managed to correct many of the mistakes of Mézeray, for which he received Voltaire's praise. Unhappily, he substituted many of his own; Boulainvilliers said they numbered in the thousands. Worse still he ignored the arts, customs, commerce, and laws of the nation, devoting most of his attention to countless narratives of battles "with a diction that was not always pure, and a style that was too weak" [XIV:61]. The last was a cardinal sin of both Mézeray and Daniel.

For Voltaire the development of history had to be both a science and an art. Liberties taken with truth were unpardonable, but a faulty and unreadable style was in many respects a greater crime; as he confided to Frederick II in 1778: "History is after all nothing more than a gazette; the most reliable is filled with falsehoods, so the only real merit it can have is that of style" [Best. 19818]. Thirty-eight years earlier he had expressed the same sentiment in a letter to d'Argenson: "A strange idea occurs to me, that is, that only dramatists are capable of injecting interest into our dry and barbarous history" [Best. 2030]. His reasoning was that history recounted the life of a people, and that the most effective way to present it was as a drama: with exposition, plot, and dénouement. This attention to the literary aspects of history should not be exaggerated, as it was by a noted Voltairean scholar who concluded: "Voltaire approached only one prose genre from a literary point of view: that was history. Everything else for him was a work of combat, propaganda or relaxation, in which the thought or amusement was of primary consideration and without order." [4]

CHARLES XII

When the material of the historian was interesting, his task from the point of view of style was thereby made easier. Voltaire's selection of Charles XII as a subject was in contradiction to his tirades against "humanistic" historians. He justified the choice on the grounds that Charles XII and Peter the Great were the two most exciting historical figures to appear on the scene in twenty centuries. Moreover, "the decision to write on him was not just for the satisfaction of relating extraordinary deeds; we thought this reading could be uesful to some princes, if perchance the book should fall into their hands" [XVI:132]. The final pages in particular clarify the philosophic lesson. Throughout the book, Voltaire had stressed the outstanding qualities of Charles XII; at the end he pointedly showed how these very qualities, pushed to the extreme, brought about the misfortune and suffering of his people and ultimately caused his death.

> He was perhaps the only man, and certainly the only king, who lived a life without any visible weakness; his virtues, worthy of heroes, became as dangerous as vices because of their immoderation. His firmness, hardened into stubbornness, caused the desolation of the Ukraine, and detained him in Turkey for five years, his liberality, degenerating into prodigality, ruined Sweden; his courage, pushed to rashness, was responsible for his death; his justice sometimes resembled cruelty; and during the last years, his authority approached tyranny. Those enviable virtues, any one of which would have immortalized another prince, spelled the ruin of his nation. . . . His life ought to teach kings how much more desirable the fruits of a peaceful government are than the glory of war [XVI: 351].

The *Histoire de Charles XII* was different from other histories in several respects. "Not a single fact was advanced without first having consulted unimpeachable sources" [XVI: 132]. The most important of his eyewitnesses was the Baron Fabrice, who for a period of seven years had been the envoy to Charles XII. Voltaire met him in 1727 and was so intrigued by the first-hand reports of the Baron that he felt impelled to write the history of Charles XII. The abundance of reliable information, however, did not prevent Voltaire from laboring over his task for ten years before the work satisfied him. Some measure of its success can be garnered from the fact that it was translated into many languages in the eighteenth century and had eight editions in London alone. In producing this stimulating book, Voltaire had followed two simple rules he was later to suggest to Nordberg, whose *History of Charles XII* he found completely unsatisfactory: the historian should not falsify truth; more important, he must not betray humanity. And in pursuing these two goals, he should avoid calumny and boredom. With regard to Nordberg's work, Voltaire sarcastically added, he could bring himself to forgive him the calumny, because it would be little read anyway, but he could not be so lenient in judging the boredom, since he had been compelled to read it.

The *Histoire de Charles XII* represents a definite break with the "classical school" of history and marks Voltaire's first effort to elevate history from chronicles of little significance to scientific and secular analyses of events. For the first time, it may safely be said, a reliable record was set forth, though it remained essentially a political biography, cast in a somewhat romantic mold. Later, the more mature historian embraced wider horizons with deeper insight, as the whole history of man became his province.

SIECLE DE LOUIS XIV

This intensified interest in history has been generally attributed to Emilie du Châtelet's dissatisfaction with the histories of the day. During the early years of his stay at Cirey, Voltaire had started to work on his *Siècle de Louis XIV*. The first chapters, intended for publication in 1739, were seized by the police. With work on the *Siècle* temporarily halted, Voltaire, encouraged by Emilie, and desirous of influencing Frederick II, embarked in 1741 on the much larger project, the *Histoire générale* (*General History*), of which the *Siècle* eventually became the final segment. What is now the Foreword to this general history was written in 1740 and addressed to Emilie. It starts: "You wish then to overcome the disgust you have for modern history since the decadence of the Roman Empire, and would like to have a general idea of the nations that exist on this earth and cause its misery" [XI: 157]. Emilie never lived to see the finished work. If she had, her distaste for history would certainly have lessened, if not altogether disappeared. By 1745 Voltaire was able to submit to the *Mercure de France* the "Nouveau Plan d'une histoire de l'esprit humain" ("New Plan for a History of the Human Mind") along with a chapter on the arts. And before leaving for Prussia in 1750, he had finished for the same journal another section of the *Histoire générale*, the "Histoire des Croisades" ("History of

the Crusades"). This progress was made in spite of the
many interruptions during his courtier years: the newly
appointed Historiographer Royal (1745) was writing dedicatory works like the "Poème de Fontenoy"; the Gentleman of the King's Bedchamber and unofficial Poet Laureate
prepared entertainment for the court; and the temporary
confidant of ministers and kings was available to undertake
diplomatic missions.

The *Siècle de Louis XIV* was completed in Prussia and
published in 1751. In Gustave Lanson's judgment, "it was a
history of first rank, as solid and exact as was possible at the
time, and embodying a method which, if not entirely satisfactory by present standards of scientific historiography,
represented nevertheless a real progress over the historical
works of his predecessors." [5] A tableau of the whole age
replaced the limited subject of Charles XII, as Voltaire attempted to ascertain what factors had made this one of the
four great periods of history, along with those of the
Golden Ages of Greece and Rome, and the Italian Renaissance of the Medici. Most of the work on the *Siècle* was
completed at Cirey. By 1738 it was well advanced, as a letter to the Abbé Dubos on October 30 [Best. 1569] of that
year informs us. In this letter he clearly defines the goals
and the method he followed in the composition of the
Siècle. The desire to delineate a history of the human mind
and its progress during one of the most fecund periods in
history is graphically set forth in Voltaire's description of
the work. He refers to the twenty chapters as tableaux of
the great happenings of the Age: "The principal characters
are in the foreground of the canvas; the crowd is in the
background." Unessential details will be sacrificed to an
over-all impressionistic effect, for "posterity will quickly
forget the details: they are the vermin that destroy great
works." Of the two hundred volumes of memoirs consulted,
he decided to use only such material as would facilitate the
presentation of a unified work, to which nothing, theoretically, would be extraneous. And he was determined "to
paint his canvas in vivid colors, to use bold and firm lines
instead of falsifying and watering down the history through
excessive verbiage as Larrey, Limiers, Lamberty, Rousset
and others had in their many volumes on Louis XIV and

the seventeenth century." [6] "God preserve me," Voltaire added in his letter to Dubos, "from employing 300 pages to write the history of Gassendi! Life is too short, time too precious to say useless things."

The material offered by the moving scenes of military exploits, so numerous and prominent in the reign of Louis XIV, were so irresistible, however, that the philosopher who hated war, the historian who belittled the endless recitations of battles, perforce succumbed to the dramatist. Quickly forgotten was the admonition in the first chapter not to expect an undue emphasis on wars; so well forgotten, in fact, that wars take up more than half of the chapters. At least he managed to present a general picture of the nation before and after the wars. What he condemned outright, after all, were the descriptions of battles per se, suitable only for the archives.

The elaborate appraisal of the consequences of wars for France may in all probability have been undertaken to cleanse a guilty conscience, as much as to assert the more important function of history. Certainly, the rather monotonous narration of the conflicts during the nineties resulted from Voltaire's instinctive attraction to the dramatic potential of battles. One has the impression that periodically Voltaire realized he had overdone it, at which point the philosopher-historian would attempt to recover lost ground by launching into disquisitions more pertinent to his professed theories on history. Nevertheless, Voltaire found it useful repeatedly to condemn internecine political maneuvers, the innocent pawns of which were always the helpless and ignorant people. The whole of Chapter 16 constitutes an onslaught on the miseries that result from this particularly senseless type of war.

Another of Voltaire's major objections to the histories of the seventeenth and early eighteenth centuries had been the too liberal use of anecdotes. Born storyteller that he was, however, Voltaire has them scattered throughout the Siècle. Conscious of the inconsistency, he tried to justify their inclusion, and on the strength of feeble pretexts he inserted four entire chapters entitled "Particularités et anecdotes"; elsewhere he included them at the rate of about one for every two pages. Notwithstanding these lapses, Voltaire's ideal remained the same—that is, to describe what characterized the century, caused revolutions, and would remain valid a hundred years later. With a clear conscience, therefore, he continued to oppose the histories of courtiers, the portrait galleries to be found in Cardinal de Retz's *Mémoires* and the error-laden *Histoire du règne de Louis XIV* (*History of the Reign of Louis XIV*) of Limiers.

By abandoning the purely chronological format in the *Siècle*, Voltaire sought greater freedom in the presentation of his material, the better to promote his ideas. The work proceeds on independent levels of development, and the result is often a bewildering fragmentation. The absence of chronology in part prevented a coherent development on the basis of causation. Equally instrumental in the failure of Voltaire to realize the full results of the newly adopted critical method of cause and effect was the lessening of his enthusiasm, the more deeply he delved into the Age of Louis XIV. Many events during the later years of Louis XIV's reign, notably the revocation of the Edict of Nantes, the Cévennes revolt, and the excesses of Jansenism, were hardly designed to contribute to the progress that Voltaire had optimistically envisaged in contemplating the period of Corneille, Molière, and Racine. The ascending pyramid that he had initially foreseen underwent a change in conformity with Voltaire's tempered enthusiasm, although he still remained a fervent admirer of the Age of Louis XIV.

To be sure, France had lagged behind England and Italy in philosophy and sciences, "but in eloquence, poetry, literature, moral philosophy, and the amenities, the French were the leaders of Europe" [XIV:539]. In view of Voltaire's preference for the fine arts over sciences, the situation appeared favorable. Corneille and Racine had elevated the art of tragedy to its pinnacle: "they had taught the nation to think, to feel, and to express itself" [XIV:-548]. Molière was indisputably the greatest writer of comedies of all time. The status of the theater alone in seventeenth-century France would thus have sufficed to glorify that century for Voltaire, for whom drama and poetry were his favorite art forms. It should be noted that the *Siècle* contains much criticism of writers and artists, and that the passage of time has corroborated Voltaire's astuteness as a critic. Personal prejudice rarely intruded to distort his literary judgments. In his comparison of Corneille and Racine, his preference for the latter's greater elegance, correctness, and poetic and psychological insight did not prevent him from appreciating the originality of Corneille in founding French tragedy. The impartiality of Voltaire's criticism is illustrated in the number of religious writers and men of genius he singled out: Fénelon for his *Télémaque* (*Telemachus*); Bossuet for the eloquence of his *Oraisons funebres* (*Funeral Orations*) and for the literary merit of his *Discours sur l'histoire universelle* (*Discourse on Universal History*); and Bourdaloue for the excellent style of his *Sermons*. Indeed, as Voltaire took inventory of the impressive list of accomplishments in seventeenth-century letters, he must have groaned, and not always inwardly, at the retrogression that was discernible in the eighteenth century.

The arts and sciences were specific facets of the nation's life, and Voltaire's goal was to record a composite picture of the epoch. The role of commerce and government was undeniable in determining the customs of the people. France, he noted, was fortunate to have had Colbert as Contrôleur-Général from 1664. Unlike Sully, whose economic measures had had the support of Henry IV's prudent policies, Colbert had to struggle valiantly to counterbalance the extravagances of Louis XIV. Nevertheless, by overcoming discouraging obstacles, Colbert had single-handedly built the merchant marine and established France's commerce on a firm footing, all the while protecting the arts. Every year of his ministry was distinguished by the establishment of a new industry. "The French are certainly indebted to him for their industry and commerce, and consequently for their opulence, the sources of which diminish in wartime but expand in times of peace" [XIV:518–519]. It was the vision and the ability to implement grandiose ideas, Voltaire said, that established Colbert's superiority over Sully, whose genius had been primarily that of a wise and economical supervisor.*

* Colbert was so farsighted in planning, that the French Senate is only now (early summer of 1965) beginning to study the possibility of updating the nation's shipping code, which has remained virtually unchanged since Colbert drafted it in 1681.

The number of times that Voltaire indicated his unhappiness with the policies and conduct of his central hero, Louis XIV, pays tribute to his historical objectivity. In his over-all view, nevertheless, the scales still weighed heavily in the king's favor; of this, Voltaire leaves no doubt: Louis XIV had abolished duels, partially reformed the laws, ordered much new construction of buildings, established the Academy of Science in 1666, and vigorously encouraged the arts. He had also, through his ministers, improved the military, the navy, the merchant marine, and commerce. One of his most constructive actions had been to order a complete census of each province (unfortunately, this was not well carried out, except in two provinces). In addition, the king had performed many good deeds; one of them was the protection he extended to James II of England, who had been dethroned by his son-in-law William III in 1688.

Many unfavorable entries had to be listed on the opposite side of the ledger: Louis XIV's pettiness; his severity against the Jansenists; a weakness for women, luxury, and extravagance of every kind; and the two that were most reprehensible: his fondness for war and his revocation of the Edict of Nantes. Voltaire magnanimously contended that the good lived on after Louis XIV, the bad remained forgotten or was offset by subsequent actions. One example of Voltaire's evaluation of an injustice perpetrated by Louis XIV will serve, however, to demonstrate the severity with which he could judge the king when the occasion demanded it. After the French armies had captured the Palatine cities, Louis XIV ordered their complete destruction, following the suggestion of his minister of war, Louvois. "Europe was horrified; the officers themselves were ashamed to execute such harsh orders" [XIV:309]. Voltaire refused to exculpate the king on the grounds that it had been Louvois' recommendation; the king was after all in a position to veto the idea. The most that Voltaire would concede was that if the king had been able to see for himself the havoc wrought or to realize the import of this command, he would certainly have countermanded it.

Notwithstanding the flaws in the *Siècle,* this work clearly prefigured modern history. To the rigorous control of documentation, critical examination, and the dramatic narration of *Charles XII*, Voltaire had added the broader philosophic sweep of the historian of civilization. No *philosophe* was better equipped in intelligence, background, and historical sense to blaze the trail in writing critical and philosophical history. In the words of Peter Gay: "If there is a political thinker for whom the second method—the analysis of his ideas through the social and historical context—is more appropriate than for Voltaire, I do not know him. His pronouncements are deeply imbedded in and sprang directly from his political experience." [7] The publication of the monumental *Essai sur les moeurs* confirmed this view; it is unquestionably the high-water mark of his historiography.

ESSAI SUR LES MOEURS

The *Essai sur l'histoire générale et sur les moeurs et l'esprit des nations,* generally referred to today as the *Essai sur les moeurs,* was originally conceived, as we have already noted, as the *Histoire générale* and appeared in fragments in 1745–1746, 1750–1751, and 1754. The full development of the *Essai* appeared in the Cramer edition of 1756, in 164 chapters. Recognizing the impossibility of an entirely definitive edition in an historical work of this magnitude, Voltaire had by 1758 begun a revision, which was published by Cramer in 1761. It contained sixteen new chapters, while the others had been materially increased. The *Philosophie de l'histoire (Philosophy of History),* published separately in 1765 and dedicated to Catherine II, was incorporated by Voltaire in 1769 as the "Introduction" of the *Essai.* The final addition of two chapters in 1775 brought the *Essai* to its present 197 chapters.

The sheer enormity of the task that Voltaire undertook single-handedly staggers the twentieth-century mind, grown accustomed to group efforts. One-man undertakings of universal or general histories were not uncommon, of course, during the seventeenth and eighteenth centuries. One such work that Voltaire must have had in mind during the writing of the *Essai* was Bossuet's *Discours,* for he chose to start his general history with Charlemagne, with whom

Bossuet had terminated his *Discours*. (The continuing conflict in Voltaire's mind between materialist and idealist elements must have permitted more approval of Bossuet than the confirmed rationalist and enemy of the Church might have cared to disclose.) What is more, the unexpected flashes of modernity discernible in the *Discours* must have delighted Voltaire—for example, Bossuet's indirect admission of the possible unreliability of divinely inspired sources, when he recommended the use of the Septuagint version of the Bible to those readers who found the Vulgate chronology insufficient to encompass all the events of history.

Voltaire's accomplishment in the *Essai* was all the more astounding in view of his diverse activities. History represented only one facet of his busy life, albeit an important one. The seriousness with which he undertook the role of historian was revealed by the stringent restrictions he imposed upon his rebellious nature in order to obtain objectivity and impartiality. Voltaire's success was confirmed by J. H. Brumfitt in these words: "In the major works, such as *Le Siècle de Louis XIV* and the *Essai sur les moeurs,* the propagandist aim is always held in check. He was proud of these works, and wanted to be able to publish them openly under his own name. This in itself meant that he had to moderate many of his criticisms." [8] Moreover, Voltaire accepted the responsibilities as well as the honor of being Historiographer Royal, witness his criticism of former Historiographers Royal such as Boileau, Racine, Mézeray, and Daniel. The last two at least had written histories, however inadequate and distorted, he asserted, but Boileau and Racine had betrayed the office by their total ineffectuality. Voltaire did not want it said of him, as it had been said of Boileau and Racine by a witty Treasury clerk, that the only thing that had been seen of them was their signatures.

The same principles of history that prevailed in the *Siècle* obtained for the *Essai,* except that the field of inquiry had been enlarged: the epochal vision of Louis XIV now assumed global proportions. Voltaire followed the same policy of demystification, emphasized the historical accuracy of the facts and events selected to delineate the spirit and progress of the peoples and nations, and as usual stressed readability and utility to mankind. This work more than any other displays genuine interest in historical problems as history; there is less visible effort to convert these problems into weapons for his crusade.

Voltaire has long been under attack, however, for an inaccuracy and bias that supposedly deprived his work of historical perspective and insight. The most systematic accounts of the errors in the *Essai* appeared in the Jesuit Nonnotte's *Erreurs de Voltaire*. In an attempt to reach a scientific assessment of the validity of the charges of Nonnotte and other critics, René Pomeau made a close study of 150 pages in four sections of the *Essai*, laboriously checking every authority and reference. There were 380 in all: of these, 319 were exact in every respect; 32 partially exact; 6 not identified; 14 had quotations rearranged; and only 9 were incorrect. The results proved Voltaire to be quite conscientious and accurate. Modern scholars with all their superior research tools often fare worse. What is more, Voltaire's accuracy increased as he approached the modern period, for which greater materials were available. This is René Pomeau's conclusion: "Voltaire is sometimes wrong; but it is a mistake to say that his text is filled with flagrant errors. It is equally false to state that he contented himself in his haste to compile facile works." [9] The copious annotations and marginalia in the books of his large library should adequately dispel the image of frivolity. He was a serious scholar, and it is no exaggeration to claim, on the basis of the authors consulted by Voltaire, many of whom were Jesuit historians like Daniel or monastic scholars like Don Calmet, that he was "more widely and surely informed than Montesquieu, who in his *Esprit des lois* employed much the same material. . . . When Voltaire does err, it is more often than not through too great a reliance on memory." [10]

One cannot deny the frequent intervention of Voltaire's personality and prejudices in this genre, as in others. After all, it was the author of *Zadig* and *Candide* who was making the all-important selection of facts and events for his histories of civilizations. Consequently, the Church as the main obstacle to progress received much attention. A man who reportedly became so ill that he had to take to his bed on the anniversary of the *Saint-Barthélemy* massacre could

hardly be expected to agree with Daniel and other Jesuit
historians that the atrocious actions on Saint Bartholomew's
Day were not premeditated, and that Charles IX's zeal in
meting out punishment to the heretics deserved the compli-
ments of Rome. Inhuman practices that were acceptable to
religiously oriented historians horrified the humanitarian.
The condemnation and slow torture of religious dissidents
by repeatedly lowering them into the flames before finally
killing them—reported as pious acts performed for the good
of the Church—were to Voltaire "examples of refined barbarity that inspired as much revulsion against the historians
who praised them as against the judges who ordered them"
[XII:265]. It is no wonder that, in discussing cannibalism,
Voltaire was prompted to say that, although cannibalism
makes one sick, "the record of humanity often produces the
same effect" [XII:389]. In the last analysis, what is today
considered to be an undue attention on Voltaire's part to
religion was dictated by the dominant role of the Church,
both temporal and spiritual, during many of the centuries
under study.

The entrenchment of the Church in the Middle Ages
accounted for the constant conflict between secular and
clerical authority. The attempts of the latter to usurp temporal power never ceased to dismay Voltaire, who firmly
believed in a separation of Church and State. A well-
known example was the famous quarrel between Philippe
le Bel and Pope Boniface VIII at the beginning of the four-
teenth century. Voltaire was annoyed by the stupidity and
docility of monarch and people alike in their acceptance of
dictation from a Church that was filled with corruption. He
did not fail to point out such instances as Jean de Médici's
elevation to cardinal at the age of 14 and pope at 37, although in this case he found much to praise in the latter's
devotion to and encouragement of the arts, the theater, and
learning when he became Pope Leo X. The support of
learning boomeranged, remarked Voltaire, since enlightened people are ineluctably less tolerant of such flagrant
abuses as Leo X's mass sale of indulgences. The enlightenment of the masses was necessarily a slow process, so difficult had it become to weaken the hold that the authority of
traditions and institutions had imposed on the naive and

credulous minds of the ignorant people. For Voltaire—worker in the Vineyard of the Lord, struggling ceaselessly to improve the lot of man, God's noblest creature—the situation often appeared as hopeless as it was deplorable.

Incredible as it may seem, Voltaire could have presented a blacker and more distorted picture of the role of the Church by utilizing unfavorable incidents from the early history of the Church; these he could easily have justified, on the other hand, had he been so inclined, regardless of the fact that his starting point was Charlemagne. Instead, he contented himself with examples of fanaticism and intolerance drawn from recent events, perhaps because their very closeness in time would give them more impact. Typical was the story of Savonarola, whom Voltaire pictures as a gifted preacher who, having explained the Apocalypse, thought of himself as a prophet. Voltaire shows satirically how he deliberately set out to attract followers, and describes the method he employed to accomplish his goal: "After it had been announced that Charles VIII planned to come to Italy, he prophesied it, and the people believed him inspired" [XII: 178]. Tragically, religious chicanery invariably led to strife and bloodshed. Rigidly held positions bred fanaticism and superstition; in turn, they begot intolerance and injustice. This, alas, was the lesson taught by history. The country of Dante, Ariosto, and Petrarch could produce the horrifying spectacle of a Dominican supporter of Savonarola and an opposing Franciscan ready to submit their bodies publicly to flames in order to establish the divine support of their fanatic claims—this between members of the same religion. "And you know," lamented Voltaire, "it has not been long since we have emerged from such darkness, and all is not enlightened yet" [XII: 180]. Had Voltaire been able to witness in the mid-twentieth century the self-immolation of religious zealots, he would be saddened by the continuing need to eradicate the commission of such insane acts under the cloak of the respectability of religion. The depressing conditions around him did not, however, destroy his natural optimism; his own century had made enough progress in almost every field of human endeavor to justify some optimism. Increasing sections of the population reflected the improved conditions, contrary to the jeremiads of Montesquieu and Rousseau. Cities were growing everywhere, and the sciences were forging ahead.

The worst period, in Voltaire's eyes, had been the Middle Ages—the barbarity and coarseness of which were repugnant to the rationalist and humanist. Voltaire's humanistic prejudices saw the start of meaningful history with the invention of the printing press by Gutenberg in the second half of the fifteenth century, and sometimes the literary critic so overshadowed the historian that he could discern little significant progress before the early seventeenth century. These lapses in historical relativity and perspective were due as much to his classical formation as to his antipathy toward the Church. The temptation has always been great, nonetheless, to denigrate the historical value of his work on the grounds of religious bias. It is certainly a gross exaggeration to see Voltaire as no less partisan than Bossuet, and Voltaire would have been justifiably shocked by the spurious reasoning of a recent critic who found Bossuet even more objective.

> One has working for him the light of reason, the other Revelation. But there is this difference, Revelation is a fixed light, independent of the person it favors, and in admitting even that it falsifies the perspectives of history, it deceives us only in the degree to which we accept it. Reason on the other hand is uncertain, vacillating, and however general it may pretend to be is an individual element that exposes one to error.[11]

Only Voltaire's satiric scalpel could properly expose the prejudice and illogicality of such a statement.

The critics who attack the irreligion of Voltaire fail to distinguish between religion and Church. It is possible to be religious without belonging to a Church, just as one can be a member of a Church, even a respected member, without necessarily being religious. "Voltaire was always obsessed with the idea of God; he believed in God deeply and sincerely." [12] With conviction and vigor he waged war on a dual front, against the Church on one side, and atheism on the other. The "hot war" of the sixties against the *infâme* saw its counterpart in the war he found himself increasingly compelled to wage against the atheistic program and doctrines of such philosophical allies as Bayle, La Mettrie, Diderot, d'Holbach, Damilaville, and d'Alembert, to name the most illustrious of the opposing camp. This latter opposition was motivated by Voltaire's practical involvement with the ethical implications of materialism and atheism rather than with the purely religious ones.

A *philosophe*, Voltaire was certain, possessed the inner checks of reason and conscience needed to live a socially moral and useful life. In theory, then, he could have agreed with Bayle's position that a society of atheists could be as virtuous as a society of religious persons, but the thought of such a principle being put into operation frightened the pragmatic Voltaire. This conflict between the empiricist and the rationalist raged continuously within Voltaire. A striking example occurs in the *Essai* when he praises China, the Confucianism of which embodied an admirable deism, as being fired by the pure and tolerant flame of natural religion. Perceiving the *philosophe* beneath the robes of the Chinese Mandarin and the Indian Brahman, Voltaire felt immediately impelled to accept their materialistic philosophy: "Many literary persons have in truth become materialists without noticeably affecting their morality, for they find virtue so necessary to man and so desirable in itself, that a knowledge of God is not required to be virtuous" [XI:179]. Thus spoke the *philosophe*, momentarily swayed by his logical aversion toward a metaphysically based ethic. God was quickly reinstated, however, when he fully realized the dangerous consequences of a Godless society.

All of Voltaire's historical background and laudable theories were betrayed by another human weakness, his propensity to confuse customs with human nature. He was too quick to believe that what was reasonable to him must be so to others. Voltaire at times seemed to place as blind a faith in common sense and reason as Rousseau did in conscience. Repeatedly Voltaire argued that the historian must accept as fact only those things that appeared most probable, their probability being determined by reason and common sense, the ultimate and infallible arbiters that were capable of overthrowing the evidence of eyewitnesses. For Voltaire, the axiom "What is not in nature is never true" drew its strength from a Natural Law that was based on the physiological oneness of man. Throughout the *Essai* there are many examples of surrender to personal prejudice; at such times, he abandoned any semblance of historical relativism. This is evident in his refusal to accept reports of travelers or other historians, on the untenable grounds that they contravened human nature and reason as he interpreted them. He summarily and unscientifically dismissed as incredible the report that "in Cochin the son of the king's sister, not his own son, inherited the crown" [XII:371]. Such a practice was unthinkable, he reasoned, for it outraged nature.

At other times, Voltaire was not above first magnifying the unreasonableness of a report and then denouncing his own version of the statement as ridiculous, although some critics have tended to exaggerate this propensity of Voltaire. Yet, as in the Herodotus story of Babylonian prostitution, Voltaire did on occasion tamper with the original version. Where Herodotus described the women prostituting themselves once a year outside the temple, Voltaire had the whole female population participate in this annual event, and by a deliberately mischievous twist had the prostitution take place inside instead of outside the temple. Nevertheless this distortion in no way alters the basic objection in Voltaire's socially oriented mind to the impropriety and outlandish nature of the action itself: "I will never persuade myself that in the most civilized city of the world all the fathers and husbands would send their daughters and wives to a public square of prostitution, or that the legislators would legalize such a traffic" [XVI:127].

VOLTAIRE'S HISTORY: A MODERN APPRAISAL

Voltaire's shortcomings as an historian are many, when he is judged by twentieth-century standards. In general, there is insufficient scaffolding and documentation. Another flaw is the lack of integration, made inevitable by his token acknowledgment of the sixteenth century and total disdain for the Middle Ages. The longer works for the most part are fragmented, sometimes static, as in the case of the *Siècle,* and the reader will frequently be surprised to see the effect precede the cause. On the whole the didacticism is much too overt and the personal intervention undisguised, especially in the numerous sections dealing with religion. Often unsatisfactory interpretations of history result from a noticeable lack of psychological insight. And Voltaire did not even succeed in ridding his work of the harangues, portraits, and anecdotes he had denounced in the "humanistic" historians. Finally, some critics extend their denunciation of his histories to include the accusation of emotional aridity. Although the last is highly arguable, many defects do exist in Voltaire's historical works, and in varying degrees. Be that as it may, his contributions as an historian are less susceptible to argument.

With Voltaire, historical studies incorporated more research, in order to distinguish truth from myth, fact from fable. Personal anecdotes and insignificant data (more suitable for archives than for history) substantially gave way to material that was better designed to illuminate the spirit of the times and mark the social progress of a nation. The principle of causation, however faultily applied, did replace the theory of divine interference, thus permitting a more critical and analytical appraisal to supplant the sycophantic recitals of princely deeds. And not of least importance was his insistence on a greater degree of literary sophistication as a way to create more interest than had been possible in the arid chronologies and forbidding biographies of the past.

Voltaire's "conception of history is closely connected with the role played by knowledge in the determination of human conduct." [13] In this he was quite modern, for he was not interested in accumulating episodes and facts, but in constructing a philosophy of life from the facts of history; in short, he sought an interpretation of the facts as related to human conduct and progress. And the most modern concept of history is just that—unless one accepts the recently advocated theory of history as a literary and esthetic evaluation of the historical facts, with which, we might add, Voltaire would have strongly disagreed, though not so much perhaps as Jean-Jacques Rousseau would have, since the latter restricted history to a recitation of facts without any personal interpretation.

Conditions in the eighteenth century were ideal for stimulating a writer like Voltaire, whose intellectual curiosity made him turn naturally to history. The Age of Enlightenment saw a shift in emphasis from the future to the present life, from God to man, and from man as an individual to man in society. The almost universal preoccupation with sciences among the educated indicated this supremacy of the terrestrial over the celestial; literature began to reflect the realism implicit in this point of view. One natural consequence was an increased interest in political problems, the solutions of which determined man's happiness on earth. The increased concern with the human condition led to a desire to know the past better in order to effect improvements for the future. In turn, the widespread interest in the outside world created a greater demand for knowledge of the little-known societies outside Europe. Voltaire was influenced by this infectious spirit of inquiry, and through his own life and work he made it the most identifying trademark of the Enlightenment.

The histories Voltaire produced were "living" and useful works, products of a man who, unlike Rousseau, could live "deliberately" only in the mainstream of life. It is superfluous to add that this opinion has not been universally shared. The nineteenth century in particular, starting with the Romantics, looked with distaste and scorn upon Voltaire and judged him harshly as a man, artist, and historian. So eminent a figure as Ernest Renan firmly believed that Voltaire had done more harm to historical studies than an invasion of barbarians, and he attributed the sharply diminished interest in history to Voltaire's historical works. The steady stream of criticism, much of it due to the personal predilections of the critics, merely tends to confirm Voltaire's modernity and viability. The critics continue to discuss and refute Voltaire, Lanson informs us, precisely because "his history admits the same criteria as ours. Herder and Michelet, Thierry and Guizot have replaced him only by continuing his work." [14] The fact that historians like Bossuet are rarely studied enough to elicit either praise or censure is their greatest condemnation. In any event, no historian before Voltaire, and indeed few since, could more appropriately have taken as a motto: "Homo sum, humani nihil a me alienum puto."

CHAPTER IV

THE DRAMATIST

AND POET

*V*oltaire's reputation as a dramatist and poet has markedly deteriorated during the twentieth century, in sharp contrast with his increasing prestige as a writer of *contes* and history. Voltaire himself would undoubtedly have attributed the greatest chance for literary immortality to his theater, whose permanent esteem would be assured by the quality of the poetry it contained. It is inconceivable to rabid anti-Voltaireans that his contemporaries—including many of his enemies, such as Fréron, Collé, Clément, and Rousseau—should have found his tragedies brilliant and his verse dazzling. Edmond Lefèbvre denounced Voltaire's tragedies in these scathing words: "One can not insist on all the stylistic faults in Voltaire's tragedies. The review would be interminable. All one can say is that there is scarcely a fault that can not be found in his works: platitude, vagueness, imprecision, redundancy, obscurity, and downright mistakes in language; everything is there." [1] Ferdinand Brunetière underlined with greater moderation a common complaint—the two-dimensional qualities of Voltaire's characters—although he inconsistently maintained that Voltaire had humanized tragedy, had made it possible for the audience to identify with the characters. The important thing is that Brunetière felt that "no one could contest Voltaire's stature as a man of the theater and dramatic author," [2] whatever one might think of his claim to the title of poet. In sharing this appreciation of Voltaire's theater, we also reject the view that his tragedies are no longer suitable for the stage and should instead be relegated to the archives of a literary museum.

The denigration of Voltaire as a dramatist and poet follows a familiar pattern. He is compared with Corneille and Racine and found inferior—a judgment that no one would contest, not even Voltaire; on this basis, his plays are summarily dismissed as worthless. If such a criterion were applied in the evaluation of other dramatists, whose works would survive the comparison? One could with greater justice ask: What dramatist up to and even during the Romantic period produced anything superior to Voltaire's tragedies? Altogether too much has been made of his own occasional implications that in one respect or another he was improving on Corneille and Racine. The truth that is evident to anyone who is familiar with Voltaire's commentaries, prefaces, and critical works is that he considered the best work of both writers to be unsurpassable, even beyond imitation.

THE DRAMATIST

To avoid the cumbersome task of discussing Voltaire simultaneously as poet and as dramatist, we shall first concentrate on the dramatic works. A clear-cut dichotomy is of course impossible, since he wrote his tragedies in verse, and as he himself so often maintained, the quality of the verse equaled in importance the ideas set forth in the plays. The discussion will be confined to his tragedies, of which there are twenty-seven (Corneille wrote twenty-one, Racine eleven), because of their manifest superiority over the comedies. Voltaire conceived of tragedy as a higher form of art than comedy, one that required greater poetic gifts; understandably, therefore, he devoted himself more seriously to this genre. Moreover, despite his wit, sense of humor, and gift for parody and burlesque, he was incapable of assuming the role of the dispassionate spectator, so as to make an adequate study of the foibles and weaknesses of humanity. Voltaire was too intimately involved, too much a part of the mainstream of activity, to permit himself the luxury of this objectivity, the indispensable prerequisite to good comedy, à la Molière. Tragedy appealed to him because it enabled him to present sympathetic and virtuous characters so inextricably caught up in the web of fate that their pain and anguish, which could not be attributed to their own eccentricities and defects, would wring tears from the audience and serve as moral lessons. In this respect, he was conforming to the trend toward didactic theater, already seen in the works of Dancourt and Destouches at the beginning of the century. This trend was supported by the critical treatises of Rapin, Le Bossu, and Dacier, who served as decisive influences in establishing the neo-classical views that dominated the first half of the eighteenth century.

The future of the French theater, envisaged by Voltaire "was to give epic elevation to tragedy by infusing a moral lesson, by portraying grandiose events, and by heightening the style." [3] Little wonder, then, that he was attracted by the English theater of the Restoration and Augustan periods. Their epic style and theory, dominated as it was by spectacle and political and religious propaganda, immensely appealed to the dramatist who was committed to heroic tragedy and intent on expressing philosophical ideas. Though France was acknowledged to be superior in tragedy, because of the near-perfection of Corneille and Racine, the robustness and dynamism of English tragedy, its preoccupation with great and stirring subjects, and its metaphorical style of poetry caused Voltaire to regard the immortal Racine by comparison as somewhat effeminate, too dedicated to the study of man instead of to political and social utility.

What are the charges usually leveled against Voltaire as a dramatist? The principal accusation is that his plays were neither worthy of the classical traditon that had been established in the seventeenth century, nor sufficiently new to initiate a new genre. To quote André Delattre, his plays were too often only "new wine in old bottles." [4] Other critics have belittled his lack of originality, asserting that his work was for the most part no more than a rehandling of plots from ancients and moderns alike. In addition, the dramatic element was lost in all the propaganda and polemics. And finally, a charge that Voltaire would have most resented: many critics find that his worst defect is the pedestrian quality of his alexandrine verse; they feel that it lacks the variety, flexibility, poetic charm and psychological depth of the alexandrines of Corneille and especially Racine. "What really kills his theater," René Pomeau informs us, "is what perhaps saves the melodramas of Victor Hugo, that is, style." [5]

The inescapable truth is that Voltaire was pre-eminently a man of the theater; it was "his primordial and permanent vocation." [6] Over a period of seventy years, from *Oedipe* (1718) to *Agathocle* (1778), he continued to write plays. For the instinctive flair that is required in order to heighten dramatic interest, Brunetière compared Voltaire with Dumas and Scribe and found him superior to Racine.[7] So great was his love for the theater that even the realization that he was inadvertently contributing to the downfall of his cherished classical ideals failed to curb his output. Voltaire's theatrical sense was sufficiently acute and his capacity for self-criticism great enough for him to be able to recognize his own faults and shortcomings. His prefaces and correspondence are filled with too many of these admissions for us to accept them as manifestations of inverted vanity, although he certainly was vain.

It was Voltaire's insatiable love of the theater that forced him to build theaters at Cirey, Tournay, Les Délices, and Ferney. His happiest hours were those spent directing, producing, and acting in those home productions. Who can erase the image of Voltaire dressed for the role of Lusignan in *Zaïre* or Zopire in *Mahomet*, hours before the scheduled performance, giving orders to his astounded servants? In the parlance of the stage he had greasepaint in his blood, not only at the superficial level of the "ham" actor, but as a serious dramatist who had the misfortune to appear on the scene at a period of transition. As a result, he was never able either to exploit fully his skills as a classical dramatist or to adapt himself completely—because of his training—to the new trend. In the preface to *Les Scythes* (*The Scythians*) of 1767, at a time when his major works for the theater had been written, he summed up his role in the theater:

> The author of *Les Scythes* has devoted himself to the development of the art of the theater. If he has not succeeded, he will at any rate have the consolation in old age of seeing his goals fulfilled by younger dramatists who will stride firmly in his footsteps, along the route he can no longer travel [VI:270].

Dogmatically minded critics should heed Paul Valéry's words of caution with regard to dismissing authors *ex cathedra* on the basis of changing literary tastes. During his talk at the Sorbonne ceremony to commemorate the 250th anniversary of Voltaire's birth, Valéry asked: "Who knows how the future will judge the Romantics? Ronsard, during Voltaire's time, was very little appreciated, and even Racine's luster seemed dimmed around 1840. In literary eternity, the most hopeless have a chance to revive." [8] The veracity of this statement finds corroboration in the fact that the immortal Shakespeare was not universally appreciated in England in the eighteenth century. Bolingbroke and Alexander Pope thought him uncouth, and it was a feeling shared by many. "Swift, for example, mentions Shakespeare only once in his writings, and Addison, in his 'An Account of the Greatest Poets,' makes no mention of him." [9] The customary condemnation of Voltaire over the past hundred years therefore should not deter one from reevaluating his work. The time is long overdue for a rehabilitation of Voltaire's status as a dramatist and as a poet.

Many of the attacks on Voltaire by unsympathetic critics do have a strong element of truth in them. No one can deny Voltaire's ambivalent position in the theater. He was both the staunchest defender of classical traditions and the most daring innovator of his time, generally more conservative in his theories than in practice. In his first tragedy, *Oedipe*, and in *Mariamne* (1724)—the last tragedy he wrote before his exposure to Shakespeare and the English stage—he was a confirmed classicist. To be sure, *Oedipe* already contained slight deviations because of Voltaire's personal views on tragedy; these are detailed in his seven "Lettres sur Oedipe" (Letters on Oedipus") and represent a critical analysis of his own *Oedipe* as well as those of Sophocles and Corneille. *Oedipe* was nonetheless essentially classical, in spite of a greater degree of realism in the death of Jocaste and a changed conception of the function of the chorus. Gustave Lanson's assertion that Voltaire's work was more "typically French in its cleverness and impertinence, in which the improbabilities and tragic gloom of the play had been adjusted to the proprieties and been enlivened by his philosophic witticism," [10] establishes his divergence from the previous spirit of classicism, not a serious infringement by Voltaire of its precepts.

Nor can it be argued that his desire to eliminate the love intrigue in *Oedipe* constituted a conscious break with tradition. On the contrary, his aim of banishing love from tragedies was based primarily on the conviction that normal treatments of love diminished the power of tragedy. The passion of a Phèdre or Hermione was admissible, even desirable as tragic material. What he objected to was the *amour galant* so frequently found in the works of Quinault (whom he nevertheless always admired), Lagrange-Chancel, Marivaux, Crébillon, Campistron, Piron, and Thomas Corneille. The Greeks, he noted, seldom used love; they found it unsuitable for their terrifying themes. What is more, the sheltered life led by women in those days diminished the importance of love as a subject for public discussion or display. In differing from the practice generally followed by Corneille and Racine, and in preferring loveless tragedies, Voltaire had authentic support at the fountainhead of tragedy.

In the "Discours sur la tragédie" ("Discourse on Tragedy"), published with *Brutus* (1730), Voltaire stated his position briefly and clearly on the use of love themes in tragedies; that position did not change substantially throughout his career:

> For love to be worthy of the tragic theater, it must play an integral role in the plot and not be an extraneous element added merely to fill out the French or English plays, most of which are too long anyway. It must be a truly tragic passion, regarded as a weakness and combatted by remorse. Such a love must either contribute directly to the misfortunes and crimes of the heroes and heroines, thereby

demonstrating its wicked power, or virtue must triumph over it to dispel any notion of its invincibility. Otherwise it reduces itself to the level of the love found in eclogues and comedies [II:324].

Alas, Voltaire complained, gallantry too often supplanted love in French tragedies, including many by his idols Corneille and Racine. In the English theater this gallantry tended to deteriorate into debauchery. On the French scene, Voltaire blamed Corneille—not Racine, as many critics of his day contended—for having set this pattern.

The experience in England has commonly been interpreted as a revelation to Voltaire: "On his return from London, what fireworks! What changes it wrought in his prejudices and practices!" [11] No doubt, an upheaval or re-evaluation of rooted prejudices did ensue, but the champion of classicism had not deserted the classical camp. In the 1729 Preface to *Oedipe*, he still remained in theory the unequivocal and unremitting classicist. He stoutly defended the unities against La Motte, insisting that one of the strongest reasons for adherence to the unities was the simplicity that almost inevitably resulted. His defense of verse against the advocacy of prose by La Motte, who unaccountably continued to write in verse, stemmed from a deeply ingrained classical prejudice. He was too great an admirer of the seventeenth century, and too much a product of the Jesuit masters of Louis-le-Grand (classicists like Father Porée), ever to consider prose superior to verse. "When La Motte calls versification a mechanical and ridiculous work, he heaps ridicule on all the great poets of antiquity as well as on all our great poets" [II:55]. For Voltaire, verse represented the highest form of art: it was essential for either the narrative or dramatic epic forms. This conviction was buttressed by such a great inclination toward and facility for poetry, that Emilie was able to write d'Argental that his friend was so ill, all he was still able to do was write verse. On the basis of theory and instinct, Voltaire likewise rejected the multiplicity of events advocated by La Motte as against the noble simplicity of the Ancients. In practice Voltaire often violated his preachings, but most of his fifty-two plays still preserved a strict fidelity to the unity of action, the most important requirement for achieving simplicity, the *sine qua non* of real tragedy.

The year following his impassioned defense of strict classicism in the 1729 Preface to *Oedipe*, Voltaire was already making slight changes. At first, these were timid; later, as he sensed the needs of the theater and the demands of the spectators, timidity yielded to ever-growing boldness. In *Brutus,* his most republican play and therefore enthusiastically revived for a short time in 1790 by the Revolutionaries,[12] Voltaire adopted red robes for the senators, so as to create a striking effect in the semicircular formation around the altar of Mars. More and more he succumbed to the spell cast over him by that barbarous genius from across the Channel whom he had learned to admire against his better judgment and in opposition to all his background. Ironically, Voltaire, the standard-bearer of classicism, was among the first to appreciate the unclassical theater of Shakespeare and after his return from England he tried to stimulate an interest in him. Few of his less classically minded contemporaries were able to overcome their French eighteenth-century bias sufficiently to discern the genius in the "absurdities" and "barbarities" of *Hamlet, Macbeth,* and *Othello*. In 1732, under the impact of *Hamlet,* Voltaire caused a sensation by introducing in *Eriphyle* the first ghost to appear on the French stage.

What Voltaire deeply admired in Shakespeare was the tragic emotion inspired by the violent and terrible actions presented on the stage. He hoped to duplicate this effect by modifying Shakespeare's historical tableaux into psychological tragedies patterned on Corneille and Racine. Voltaire's difficulty lay in his inability to understand and appreciate the psychological studies within Shakespeare's tragedies; he had trouble enough appreciating the subtle psychological analyses of Racine. Quite erroneously, he attributed the undeniably tragic emotions experienced by the spectators of Shakespeare's tragedies to the rapidity of action and the boldness and horror of the spectacle. Voltaire was transfixed by the appearance of Brutus, still holding the dagger dripping with Caesar's blood, as he stood on the tribune attempting to justify the assassination of his friend to the assembled Romans. To approach perfection, Voltaire thought, all he had to do was to combine this type of dynamism with French taste and correctness. His efforts were foredoomed to partial failure. Instead of being able to prolong classicism in a more revived form, he was confronted with the necessity "to soften the passion, civilize the tragic hero, substitute chance for fatality and the pathetic for the tragic." [13] Unwittingly, he served as a catalyst, helping to mold public taste when he did not yield to it, and inexorably bridging the gap between Shakespeare and Racine.

At first his innovations greatly shocked his audiences, even though he was careful to present his material within a Racinian envelope. Up to the first part of the eighteenth century little attention had been given to the staging of plays. "Settings, costumes, and accessories seemed superfluous and unimportant nonsense to the actors and writers of tragedies." [14] Against this background, the institution of change had to be accomplished slowly, or as in Voltaire's case, by the tactical adoption of alternating boldness with retreat, a pattern of vacillation that betrayed the constantly warring elements within him: on the one hand, the attunement to audience reaction; on the other, the inescapable inner restraints imposed by classicism. *Zaïre* in 1732 revealed this strange mixture of the old and new. It was the first play in which he dared to give full rein to his sentiment. In writing *Zaïre*, he yielded to the numerous complaints from women who had protested against the absence of love in his plays. Equally important, he desired an outstanding achievement in the theater such as had eluded him since the triumph of *Oedipe*. After the resounding success of *Zaïre*, Voltaire reverted to his original belief that love was more appropriate to comedy than to tragedy, although he still found it expedient to incorporate a love theme in many of his later plays. Another innovation in *Zaïre* was the use of French characters, a practice not at that time in vogue. And whether this is attributable to the influence of the English theater, to Voltaire's natural inclination for spectacle, or to his recognition that changes were in order, *Zaïre* does present more action, thereby setting a quicker pace, which sometimes strains the verisimilitude of the play. There were also more *coups de théâtre* and typical Molière "recognition scenes." His fondness for history came to the fore in his quest for more local color through greater faithfulness to the customs of the Orient. Fortunately, he was enough of a dramatist to realize that a tragedy is not a history, and too much of a classicist to pursue historical authenticity to the point of impairing the dramatic interest of the play.

On the other hand, the unities are respected. *Zaïre* has the traditional five acts, and there are no comic elements. The treatment of passion in Orosmane, and the conflict between love and religion in Zaïre are Racinian in quality. Indeed, it is not difficult to see something of Racine's Pyrrhus in Orosmane; Zaïre does not resemble closely the typical heroines of either Corneille or Racine: her love is more passionate and psychologically true than that of Corneille's heroines, yet it is not the raging passion of a Phèdre. In 1732 it was still inadvisable to have Orosmane stab Zaïre onstage; just before the dagger struck her, therefore, she managed to reach the wings. Suicides being permitted, however, by the rules of decorum (a distinction that Voltaire never understood), Orosmane was able to kill himself in full view without shocking the audience.

On the whole the spectators welcomed more action and spectacle to replace the often tiresome and interminable speeches. Cliques were, of course, always ready to boo and hiss changes, particularly when their primary intent was to deny the author a triumph. *Adélaïde du Guesclin* in 1734 suffered such a fate. Voltaire had, during the previous year, published his *Temple du Goût* (*Temple of Taste*) and made many enemies by the bold criticism of some of the cherished names in French literature. As a result, his enemies seized upon the opportunities offered by the startling theatricalism in *Adélaïde* so as to insure its downfall and to force Voltaire to withdraw it. The classical diehards and those who sought excuses to topple the play objected strenuously to actions such as Nemours' entrance, arm in sling and covered with blood, and the cannon-shot at the end, notifying Vendôme that his brother Nemours had been executed. It is interesting to note that a reworked three-act version of the play, the *Duc d'Alençon*, was presented successfully at Potsdam in 1751. The following year another version, the *Duc de Foix*, was given in Paris without the bloody face, the visible wounds, and the cannon-shot. Since the incomparable Lekain played the part of Vendôme, the play was well-received. By 1765, when the original version was again presented in Paris, this time with great success, the audiences had not only become accustomed to deviations from classical theater, they actually clamored for visual entertainment. The composition of the audience had meantime undergone a change; the opinion of the literate and critical spectators no longer prevailed.[15]

The public no longer admired the theater of Corneille and Racine, because its appeal to the mind and emotions was almost exclusively aural. Audiences were insisting increasingly on the aural being supplemented by the visual. The simple costume change in *Brutus* (1730) that had seemed so daring at the time had become in *Orphelin de la Chine* (*Chinese Orphan*, 1755) a major costume innovation, designed to reproduce the spirit and customs of the Orient. The added visual effects enabled *Orphelin* and other plays to compete more favorably with the ever-increasing popularity of the spectaculars that were being staged at the Opera. This campaign in costume changes, which had been initiated by Lekain and Mlle. Clairon, was carried to total victory by Talma in the 1789 production of *Brutus*. Playing the part of Proculus, he appeared in a real Roman toga, with arms and legs bare and without powdered hair. The resistance that is offered by tradition has to be eliminated gradually before victory can be achieved. In 1732 Voltaire had Eriphyle duel and die in the wings, a propriety adhered to in *Zaïre* (1732) and *La Mort de César* (*The Death of Caesar*, 1735). By 1741 in *Mahomet* he pushed temerity to its limit by having Zopire killed on the stage; and to make the change more startling, Zopire was assassinated by his own son, Séide, although of course, Séide did not at the time know that Zopire was his father.

After *Mahomet*, Voltaire returned with a vengeance to his strict classical principles in *Mérope* (1743)—without doubt his purest tragedy, the simplest in construction, and completely devoid of a love plot and propaganda. For those who are incapable of forgetting Racine when they are studying Voltaire, the purity of the plot is marred by Voltaire's habit of not starting the action, as Racine would have, *in medias res*. The need to prepare the dénouement forced him to create secondary lines of interest, even in his most classical play, *Mérope*.[16]

After *Mérope*, *Sémiramis* (1748) returns to the more familiar form of *coups de théâtre*, a spectacle that all but destroyed the classical conception of unity of place. Among the striking scenes are the gathering of the powerful elements of the city for the betrothal announcement by Sémiramis, and the appearance of the ghost of Ninus to the accompaniment of thunder claps and the shaking of the tomb. Probably the most dramatic scene resulted from what Voltaire termed the *colin-maillard du tombeau* ("blindman's buff in the tomb"). Arzace, having learned from the high priest Oroès that he was Ninias, the son of Ninus, and that Assur had killed his father, went into the tomb to kill Assur. Inadvertently he stabbed his mother, Sémiramis, who had preceded Ninias into the tomb to protect him from Assur. Nothing in the tragic theater of the first half of the eighteenth century equals in magnetic power and sheer horror the appearance of the fatally wounded Sémiramis, staggering out of the tomb under the horrified gaze of her grief-stricken son. The hypnotic fascination of that scene surpasses the poignant moment when Séide assassinates Zopire.

During Voltaire's lifetime, few plays enjoyed greater success than *Orphelin de la Chine*. Originally written in three acts, like *La Mort de César*, it was rewritten into five acts only at the insistence of d'Argental, who feared that the abandonment of the classical five-act structure would place in jeopardy the success of the play. The correspondence between the two indicates that Voltaire complied very reluctantly, his dramatic sixth sense probably assuring him that audiences were now ready to accept what they would have found shocking twenty years before. Voltaire's art of "speaking to the eyes" is best exemplified by this play. Drawing the subject from his research for his *Histoire universelle*, he gave the audiences their fill of local color by transporting them with much authenticity to the China of Genghis Khan. Once again the superlative acting of Mlle. Clairon and Lekain contributed substantially, as did their

insistence upon wearing costumes different from those tra-
ditionally worn. More radical still, Mlle. Clairon had argued for the adoption of natural and simple diction in place
of the stilted declamation then in vogue. With the changes
in costume, Voltaire had no disagreement; he himself had
made similar suggestions as early as 1730 in the "Discours
sur la tragédie." As for the change in diction, he once again
betrayed the conflict, always seething just below the surface,
between his willingness to experiment and his classical
reluctance to renounce the past. The universal acclaim received by the play momentarily allayed Voltaire's mis-
givings.

Many years after the success of *Orphelin*, in the Preface
to *Les Scythes*, Voltaire once again reverted to his old conviction, firmly expressed in his "Dissertation sur la tragédie
ancienne et moderne" ("Dissertation on Ancient and Modern Tragedy," 1748), that the magnificence of classical declamation should be retained. He bitterly complained that
"Actors were beginning to pride themselves on speaking
their lines as though they were prose" [IV:498]. The reit-
eration of these views in 1767 was less understandable, for
Les Scythes featured shepherds and contrasted simple
agrarian customs with those of the pomp and luxury of ori-
ental courts. The justification for simple, unaffected diction
was therefore even greater as a way of giving the play the
verisimilitude he had always insisted a play should have.
Nevertheless, Voltaire's complaint was essentially the same:
"the miserable manner of reciting verse like prose, of failing
to appreciate its rhythm and harmony, has almost destroyed
the art of declamation" [VI:270].

The modern side of Voltaire, his predilection for spectacle, could not be fully exploited, however, until after the
stage was finally rid of the spectators, who had previously
impeded the action of the play and restricted the possibili-
ties of dramatist and actors alike. For years Voltaire had
deplored this custom, which had started in 1636 with the
full houses for *Le Cid* and had persisted for more than a
century as an unchallenged tradition (a sinister word to
Voltaire when it had to do with something he found objectionable). In the "Dissertation sur la tragédie ancienne et
moderne" he had decried the absence of good theaters in

which to mount satisfactory productions, and had likewise noted: "one of the greatest obstacles to the presentation of any grand and moving action in our theaters is the crowd of spectators mingled pell-mell on the stage with the actors" [IV:499]. Many years earlier, in a letter to the Abbé Desfontaines, November 14, 1735, Voltaire had complained: "Our theater lacks action and interest for the spectators. The lack of action is the direct result of a stage cluttered with *petits-maîtres*" [Best. 909]. In 1759, Lauraguais managed to clear the stage by paying the sum of 60,000 francs to compensate for the places on the stage. The delighted Voltaire produced *Tancrède* (1760), his first play to utilize the full stage. He was so grateful that in the same year he dedicated the comedy, *L'Ecossaise,* to Lauraguais.

The tradition persists that Voltaire used crossed rhymes in *Tancrède* in order to avoid being recognized as the author. The truth is more likely "that Voltaire's use of alternating rhyme in *Tancrède,* giving a more rapid and conversational effect than was possible in alexandrines, was impelled by Diderot's charge that verse stood between the spectator and the dramatic actor." [17] This departure from classical verse disturbed Voltaire, as his dedicatory letter to Mme. de Pompadour reveals: "The kind of verse I used in *Tancrède* approaches prose too much, I fear. It could thus happen that, in wanting to improve the French stage, I might ruin it completely" [V:498]. But *Tancrède* enjoyed a tremendous success, in large part due to Mlle. Clairon and Lekain, who often insured the success of Voltaire's plays with their brilliant acting. Had Voltaire been more alert to the danger signals he himself had indicated in the "Discours sur la tragédie," which he addressed to Milord Bolingbroke in 1730, he might have suspected the presence of inherent weaknesses in his plays. Addison's *Cato,* he had reminded Bolingbroke, owed its greatness only to the beautiful lines, which presented true and powerful thoughts expressed in harmonious verse. When a play depended upon externals to insure its popularity, that invariably denoted a mediocre play, even though the audiences wept and enjoyed themselves during the performances. This type of transitory success misled authors into believing that their works were brilliant, and they congratulated themselves in prefaces on the magnificence of their plays. One wonders how much of Voltaire's extraordinary fame as a dramatist in the eighteenth century depended upon the rendition of his lines by Mlle. Clairon and Lekain instead of on the lines themselves. *Tancrède*, for example, enjoyed after *Zaïre* the greatest acclaim of all his plays. When it is read, the play's vapid exposition and monotonous speeches scarcely seem to warrant the reception it received.

The height of Voltaire's daring in his quest for dramatic effects was reached with *Olympie* (1763), in which the heroine throws herself into the flaming pyre of her mother, Statira, in full view of the spectators. Statira's last wish had been that Olympia marry Antigonus instead of Cassandre, who had killed Olympia's father, King Alexander. Unable either to stop loving Cassandre or to disobey her mother, Olympia resolved her dilemma by killing herself. One night this extraordinary touch of realism almost set fire to the theater. In *Olympie*, which is in effect a continual tableau, Voltaire circumvented the restricting conventions of the classical stage, as he did in many other plays, by having a curtain backstage open to reveal another setting: in *Olympie*, the funeral pyre of Statira; in *Mahomet*, Zopire praying at the altar; in *La Mort de César* the dead body of Caesar. The same device was used in *Eriphyle, Brutus, Alzire*, and *Mérope*. In some plays he quite openly changes scenes, though as unobtrusively as possible; three times in *Sémiramis*, and twice in both *Tancrède* and *Rome sauvée* (*Rome Saved*).

More and more Voltaire yielded to the temptation to present melodramatic and spectacular scenes. The recently cleared stage permitted such whims, and the audiences, imbued with the strong currents of sentiment that pervaded the second half of the eighteenth century, encouraged them. He took liberties that would have dismayed the author of *Mérope*. What is worse, second-rate writers, such as Ducis, Du Belloy, and Lemierre, proceeded to extend with inartistic boldness Voltaire's innovations. Spurred on by the enthusiastic reaction of the spectators, and having none of the built-in checks of the classically inspired Voltaire, they inundated the stage with plays that made a shambles of classical form and style. Just as political events leading to the cataclysmic Revolution exceeded the political theories of the *philosophes,* so did the literary evolution rout the classical standards of the past. With some justice, critics like Gustave Lanson blamed Voltaire for having destroyed tragedy by his very efforts to improve it.[18] Too severe a condemnation of Voltaire overlooks a point generally made by these same critics—that is, that the classical theater of the seventeenth and early eighteenth centuries simply had to undergo modifications in order to conform to the changing times. Moreover, an inconsistency presents itself when critics on the one hand excoriate Voltaire for altering the classical concepts and on the other hand condemn his tragedies as being no longer meaningful, on the grounds that the alexandrine verse and the classical format, which hark back to a bygone era, have gone out of fashion and are therefore no longer acceptable. Regardless of the merit of these reservations, it should be remembered that Voltaire himself seldom flagrantly violated the basic unities, and his theoretical statements on the theater consistently defended what he called the "fundamental rules of the theater"—the classical unities of time, place and action. The changes he sought to implement, and which he strove to make acceptable to French audiences, involved minor rules of decorum —such things as the prohibition of bloody scenes on the stage, the impossibility of having more than three speaking characters on the stage at one time, and the necessity for the author to develop every plot within a five-act format. These minor changes in themselves did constitute an impressive shift from the classical concept of the theater, all the more remarkable since he was the most highly respected practitioner of the art of writing for the theater; they scarcely justify a general stigmatization of the tragedies of Voltaire.

The complaint that Voltaire's plays are filled with propaganda is substantially true, although "didacticism" might be a better word than "propaganda," with its pejorative connotations. Critics differ on this point, as in everything else. John Morley contends that with Voltaire, tragedy is, as all art ought to be, a manner of disinterested presentation. [19] Ronald R. Ridgway, in a detailed study of the philosophical propaganda in Voltaire's tragedies, reached the reasonable conclusion that it is ridiculous to speak of art for art's sake in connection with Voltaire's theater.[20] With Raymond Naves, he hypothesized that Voltaire had greater faith in his messages than in the plays themselves; he cited Voltaire's efforts to secure the Pope's approval of *Mahomet* as proof of the importance he attached to his theatrical propaganda. It is much more likely that Voltaire behaved as most dramatists would have under similar circumstances, simply in order to assure the production of the play.

Voltaire's last message to Pope Benedict XIV, congratulating him on his profound knowledge of Virgil, is in itself a masterpiece of irony. The Pope, one will recall, had refuted a French writer's censure of Voltaire's use of "hic" in a Latin distich addressed to the Pope. The latter had displayed an unusual degree of vanity in recounting his literary triumph. In his reply Voltaire maliciously inserted this observation: "Veramente sono in obbligo di riconoscere la sua infallibilità nelle decisioni di letterature, siccome nelle altre cose più riverende" ("Truly I am obliged to recognize your infallibility in literary decisions as well as in other more reverend matters") [IV:104]. Voltaire, the eternal fighter and in this case the inveterate dramatist, was determined to win the struggle with Crébillon, who was preventing the presentation of the play. In order to do this, he was prepared to use the whole arsenal of Voltairean weapons—which included deceit, hypocrisy, and downright lies. He would probably have acted the same way had there not been the slightest iota of propaganda in the play.

To be sure, all of Voltaire's works reflected his humanistic impulse to instruct his fellowman and to improve his lot. In Norman L. Torrey's words: "There was no trace of 'art for art's sake' in his literary theories, and except in a very few of his plays Dame Literature bent the knee to Dame Philosophy." [21] From this, however, to the contention that all his poetic works, including his plays, are pamphlets in disguise is an unwarranted leap. Some plays are remarkably free of any obvious pamphleteering. Where the presence of the polemicist and propagandist is apparent, the justification is simply that religion played a dominant role in every aspect of eighteenth-century life.

A noted critic contends that "the tragedies are among the richest sources of Voltaire's philosophy," [22] despite the fact that the dramatic format offered Voltaire less flexibility than the *contes* and histories. The definite advantage this medium offered lay in its concretization and personalization of philosophic ideas—that is, the stage was capable of placing philosophy within a setting of human experience. A message could be forcefully driven home in the form of the dire consequences of a character's unethical conduct being unfolded before the spectator's eyes. At times, Voltaire resorted to the less artistic method of stating his message directly, as he did at the end of *Sémiramis* (1748) when the high priest of Oroès intones:

> Par ce terrible exemple apprenez tous du moins
> Que les crimes secrets ont les dieux pour témoins.
> Plus le coupable est grand, plus grand est le supplice.
> Rois, tremblez sur le trône, et craignez leur justice
>
> [IV:567].*

When Voltaire was not trying in so forthright a manner to influence rulers to wield their authority with justice, he sought the same result indirectly by minimizing the power of religion over the monarch. This is evident from his very first play *Oedipe*, in which one finds these oft-quoted lines of Jocaste:

> Nos prêtres ne sont point ce qu'un vain peuple pense
> Notre crédulité fait toute leur science.
>
> *Our priests are not what people think*
> *It is our credulity that gives them all their power and skill*
>
> [II:93].

As an exception, a play such as *Mérope* will contain little or no propaganda. *Zaïre,* on the other hand, can easily be interpreted as a condemnation of too rigid emphasis on religious externals by Lusignan and Nérestan. Their demands create the indecision and uncertainty in the mind of Zaïre that eventually serve to awaken the jealousy of Orosmane and lead to the tragic death of Zaïre and the suicide of Orosmane, two persons deeply in love with each other.

* Freely translated, this reads: "By this terrible example, may all at least learn that secret crimes have the gods as witnesses. The higher the position of the guilty party, the greater the punishment. Kings, tremble on your thrones and fear their justice!"

Mahomet is more openly a diatribe against superstition and fanaticism, the frightful dangers and inhumanity of which are exemplified in Séide, who became the tool and victim of an unprincipled and ambitious religious impostor, Mahomet. The stage, as Voltaire had told Mme. de Pompadour in the "Dedicatory Epistle" of *Tancrède,* should always represent "an ever-continuing school of poetry and virtue" [V:496].

Voltaire was a consummate craftsman in the working out of ideas as guidelines for men's actions. No one knew better than he that ideas were rendered most effective by being couched in a social frame rather than an abstract dialectic. "In brief, the testing of ideas in terms of their meaning within a setting of human experience is the philosophic technique involved in Voltaire's procedure of presenting certain ideas to a specific audience by means of various literary vehicles." [23] The pertinent question is whether the dramatic and literary qualities of a play are vitiated because the dramatist has incorporated a message or highlighted a problem of the day. Is there any great work of literature that is without a message for the reader or spectator? Does Euripides' *The Trojan Women* lose any of its dramatic power or literary value because it is a sublimely eloquent, symbolic protest against the savage treatment of Melos by his fellow-Athenians? The conviction of an eminent authority is that "apart from the vast superiority of the Greek in depth and passion and dramatic invention, in Voltaire this philosophising is very much more indirect, insinuatory, and furtive, than in the marked sententiousness of Euripides." [24] To bring the question up-to-date, is *Les Mouches* (*The Flies*) of Jean-Paul Sartre any the less literature because of its easily recognizable message to the readers of occupied France? For many twentieth-century critics of the new school, the increase of emphasis on style over content has minimized the importance of ideas; some would even claim ideas to be unworthy of serious literary study. The test of time will surely rectify this restricted view and the audience will expect of all imperishable works of literature a respected place for ideas alongside skills of style. Surely Voltaire would approve.

If critics are justified in condemning Voltaire's plays for

their ideas, then all his works are doomed to the same fate, including those universally acclaimed masterpieces, *Candide* and *Zadig*, because they preach far more effectively than does any tragedy of Voltaire. The stock answer that the propaganda in the tragedies is too obvious and too intrusive is not tenable. The tragedies that deserve to be rescued from oblivion—*Oedipe, Zaïre, Adélaïde du Guesclin, Alzire, Mahomet, Mérope, Sémiramis,* and *Tancrède*—can all be read and seen without one's being unduly aware of their "message." Naturally, it may appear "obtrusive" to the knowledgeable student of Voltaire, who is consciously seeking the presence of a message.

Nor can one take too seriously the accusation that Voltaire's theater lacked originality, that all he did was "to follow gloriously in the footsteps of others," in the phrase of his inveterate enemy Fréron who, as Favart's letter to Durazzo of September 7, 1760 informs us, was preparing a six-volume work to document this charge. Reputable scholars find that "his works as much as those of any man who ever lived and thought are truly his own." [25] The influence of Shakespeare should not be exaggerated; the resemblances are for the most part superficial. With much force and cogency Trusten W. Russell argues that "in regard to English drama his ties were with the Restoration and Augustan theaters, not with Shakespeare, and that, finally, in such plays as *Zaïre, Alzire,* and *Tancrède* he was actually very close to the heroic formula of Dryden, whose example, the evidence indicates, was particularly useful." [26] Two aspects of the English theater appealed to Voltaire: first, its capacity to arouse pity and terror, to stir the emotions with violent, terrifying, even horrifying actions; second, and what was probably more appealing to him, was its tendency to discuss philosophical ideas.

In 1728, while in England, he wrote "Essai sur la poésie épique" ("Essay on Epic Poetry") as an Introduction to *La Henriade.* In this work of criticism, originally written in English, this statement appears: "In England, tragedy is really an action; and if the authors of this country joined to the activity which enlivens their plays a natural style combining decency and regularity, they would soon surpass both the Greeks and the French" [VIII:307]. He himself

made a valiant and conscious effort—too successful, as it
turned out, for the survival of classicism—to incorporate
these facets of the English theater. On the whole, Voltaire
experimented within the main tenets of the French classical
theater. Even *Zaïre*, the play most associated with Shakespeare because of its resemblance to *Othello*, is completely
French; it is different in so many fundamental respects
from the source of its inspiration that a serious comparison
would be unwarranted.

Sometimes Voltaire's own ingenuousness—if this word
can properly be used to describe so worldly and mercurial a
person—furnished critics with the grounds upon which they
were able to build a *prima facie* case against him of plagia-
rism or unscrupulous borrowing. A notable example is that
of *Mérope*. In a long letter to Maffei, Voltaire candidly
admitted having been so moved by the 1733 Paris performance of Maffei's *Mérope*, at which he had had the opportunity to make the author's acquaintance, that he decided to
translate it. Critics seized upon this admission by Voltaire
to substantiate their own accusations, which placed his
honesty and originality in question. They failed to take into
account what actually took place. Having found himself
unable to adjust many of the actions of the Italian *Mérope*
to the French proprieties and customs, Voltaire confessed
that he had had to abandon the project: "I was obliged
regretfully to write a new *Mérope*; I did it differently, but I
am far from believing that it is better" [IV: 189]. Accusations, like slander and rumor, have a tendency to snowball.
He was accused of copying not only Maffei, but Racine's
Andromaque and Lagrange-Chancel's *Amasis* as well. Lessing, motivated by personal animosity and a desire to build
up the German theater, willingly joined the pack at Voltaire's heels. Henri Lion, however, who made a careful
study of this matter in his comprehensive Sorbonne dissertation, *Les Tragédies et les théories dramatiques de Voltaire* (*Voltaire's Tragedies and His Dramatic Theories*,
1895), found no truth in the charges. What resemblances did exist were superficial at best. In the flurry of
charges, Voltaire remained his irrepressible self, as a letter
to Mlle. Quinault reveals: "*Mérope* resembles *Amasis* because it has a mother; it resembles *Gustave Vasa*, because

it has a son; it resembles nothing because it has no love" [Best. 1399].

The devaluation of Voltaire's theater on the basis of the argument that he borrowed many of his subjects from the Ancients raises the interesting speculation of the effect this type of assessment would have had on Corneille, Molière, and Racine, to list the three most respected French dramatic writers. Their plays frequently used subjects that had been treated by the Greeks and Romans. This practice of reworking familiar themes is still in vogue—the Théâtre National Populaire in Paris recently showed Jean-Paul Sartre's new version of *The Trojan Women*. In Voltaire's day, one must remember, it was a common practice, one that was encouraged and applauded, except by the author's enemies, for it was seen as a challenge: "An author requires as much inventive genius to rewrite *Oedipe* or *Mérope* after numerous treatments of the subjects as he would need to imagine an entirely new tragedy." [27] Furthermore, a study of Voltaire's plays reveals that the number of subjects borrowed from his predecessors is less than one would at first be led to believe. The repetitious quality of his work is also misleading; it can in part be attributed to his penchant for recasting or reworking the same plays and to his habit of inserting parts of unsuccessful plays into new plays.

It has always been the fate of Voltaire to be misjudged. In the theater he has been attacked for being too much of an innovator and for lacking originality. Yet, his contribution to the theater was clearly more significant than that of any other eighteenth-century dramatist. Pointing to the novelties in *Brutus, Eriphyle, Zaïre, Adélaïde du Guesclin, La Mort de César*, and *Alzire*, Gustave Lanson explained that no one could have appealed in a more striking way to the French mind and spirit. Later, Voltaire made greater use of distant and exotic settings, to the extent that his own interest in universal history increased. The subjects drawn from his historical research and dramatically treated in *Adélaïde, Alzire*, and *Orphelin* had never before been used in tragedies. The meaningful comparisons of different cultures must certainly rank as one of Voltaire's outstanding contributions to the theater.

Concentrating as he did on foreign locales and exotic customs, Voltaire, without intention, introduced the element of local color that was to become so dear to the Romantics. The consensus of several critics is that Voltaire did make possible the triumph of the Romantic drama. The scorn for Voltaire that the Romantics exhibited consequently represents another classic example of injustice and irony, since he had served as a bridge between classicism and the melodrama that preceded the development of the more artistic and philosophical plays of the Romantic era. The statistics furnished by Gustave Lanson convincingly support this contention. When one compares him with Corneille and Racine, the number of presentations of Voltaire's works at the Comédie Française, according to the official statistics of the theater, show that in 1763 there were 16 for Corneille, 17 for Racine, and 48 for Voltaire. For 1775 the figures were Corneille 10, Racine 20, and 54 for Voltaire. The year of the Revolution, it was Corneille 18, Racine 28, and Voltaire 42. The neo-classical period saw Voltaire's popularity temporarily lag behind; in 1805 the figures were Corneille 57, Racine 59, and only 28 for Voltaire. In 1828, the previous trend had reasserted itself with 9 for Corneille and 26 for Racine, while Voltaire remained constant at 28. [28] These statistics eloquently reveal the vogue that was enjoyed by Voltaire during the pre-Romantic period, an honor that our classically trained dramatist might not perhaps have cherished.

Voltaire did not realize until late in life to what a great extent he was personally responsible for the changes in the theater. In 1769, after the successful presentation of *Hamlet* in Paris, he wrote d'Argental:

> I modestly opened the way; now others are plunging ahead at breakneck speed—*domandavo acqua, non tempesta* [I was asking for water, not a flood]. I wanted to insert some life into the theater by adding more action, and now all we have are action and pantomime. There is nothing sacred enough to be safe from abuse. In everything we are heading for extremes and grotesqueness [Best. 14963].

In truth, thanks to Voltaire's example and preachings, and to some extent the influence of Crébillon and Ducis, tragedy had become, in the hands of less capable artists, "a sort of tragedy tailored to the taste of the masses." [29] Crébillon had contributed horror and complicated plots; Ducis, in his translations of Shakespeare, violent scenes and pantomime; Voltaire, animated action and recognition scenes. The popularity of the melodramas at the boulevard theaters helped to perpetuate many of these traits in the Romantic theater.

Years later, his *mea culpa* was expressed with greater anguish and despair. This occurred in 1776, after the publication of Letourneur's translation of Shakespeare, in the preface of which he denounced the French for having overlooked and failed to appreciate Shakespeare. In the "Lettre de M. de Voltaire à l'Académie Française" ("M. Voltaire's Letter to the French Academy"), quickly dispatched to d'Alembert, the Secretary of the Academy, he indignantly protested the inaccuracies of Letourneur [see XXX:351]. What really aroused Voltaire's ire, as his letter to d'Argental that same year indicates [Best. 19082], was Letourneur's categoric dismissal and disparagement of Corneille and Racine.

Voltaire's diatribe was neither the result of piqued vanity nor the expression of his true feelings about Shakespeare. It was a troubled conscience finally brought face to face with the consequences of its actions. The classicist whose literary ideal resided in the Golden Age of Louis XIV had been suddenly compelled to assess himself and his achievement. What he saw was a man who was, perhaps, "too much in tune with his times," who had mistaken the eighteenth-century tendency to elicit tears for the evocation of pity and terror by tragedy. Inadvertently, he had slipped into the mold more suited to Richardson, Diderot, La Chaussée, Greuze, Jean-Jacques Rousseau, and Bernardin de Saint-Pierre. It was this great appeal to the surface emotions, typical of most melodramas and Romantic plays, that explains in part why many of his tragedies were warmly received on the stage.

THE POET

To attribute the failure of Voltaire's plays to the mediocrity of the poetry seems preposterous on the surface, if one takes into account the respect and admiration that Europe had for his poetic genius. The scorn of modern critics for the poetic value of his alexandrine verse—for the moment, the discussion will be confined to the poetry of his tragedies —was inevitable when tastes changed. The ponderous march of the stately alexandrine has lost its appeal for the modern ear; its order and restraint have become somewhat alien to our temperament, and rhyme itself has gone out of fashion. To make matters worse, most studies of Voltaire's plays have so overemphasized the importance of spectacle and action, that both the friend and the foe of Voltaire receive the impression that he was primarily if not exclusively interested in visual appeal and the entertainment of his audiences. As sympathetic and astute a critic as Raymond Naves has asserted: "he was interested only in the conduct of the action and spectacle." [30] Nothing could be further from the truth, as he repeatedly tells us in his many prefaces and discourses. If someone had asked Voltaire to describe himself, he would undoubtedly have answered that he was a poet.

The vast correspondence (some 20,000 letters) offers innumerable examples of the ease with which he would lapse into verse. But verse is not poetry, the anti-Voltaireans retort. Voltaire's use of rhyme, facile and expert though it was, does not transform rational, philosophic, and prosaically ordered lines into poetry! How startling a discovery it would be to such critics to learn that Voltaire was as adamant on this point as they. He often expressed his scorn for the prosaic maker of rhymes, and nowhere more forcefully and explicitly than in the seven "Lettres sur Oedipe." Part of the fifth letter reads: "I can not tolerate the sacrifice of all the other beauties of poetry to the richness of rhyme, nor can I accept the desire to please the ear instead of the heart and mind" [II:41]. In these comments on rhyme, Voltaire made it clear that the ability to construct rhymes did not serve to transform a prose writer into a poet, nor was rhyme the poetic ingredient that *ipso facto* guaranteed the greatest pleasure for the reader. It is noteworthy that in his letter of December 20, 1737 to Frederick II [Best. 1346], answering a request for some simple rules to differentiate poetry from prose, Voltaire did not include rhyme.

Whatever the prevailing prescription for poetry may be in the ever-changing tastes of succeeding generations, harmony and rhythm—with or without rhyme—and thought —with or without imagery—are the principal ingredients of poetry. And no one in the eighteenth century was more concerned than Voltaire with the harmony and rhythm of his lines, a preoccupation that in fact extended into his prose-writing. That is why he protested so often and so bitterly against the restrictions artificially imposed by traditions and those inherent in the French language itself.

The English and the Italians were more fortunate; their languages enabled them to dispense with rhyme because of the liberties and inversions permissible in English and Italian that were either impossible or very difficult in French poetry. Having tasted the freedom of English blank verse, he confessed that he himself preferred the liberties that it afforded the poet, since thought was more important to him than rhyme. The rules of French versification, complained Voltaire, handicap the poet. They force him "to write four lines of poetry to express a thought that an Englishman can render in a single line. The Englishman can thus say all that he wishes; the Frenchman, only what he can" [II:312]. It was precisely the inherent weaknesses of the French language, argued Voltaire, that necessitated the retention of rhyme as an indispensable crutch. To compound the difficulties confronting the eighteenth-century poet, the great poets like Corneille, Racine, and Despréaux had so accustomed French ears to rhyme that anyone "who freed himself of the burden supported by the great Corneille would be regarded with reason not as a bold genius who blazes a new trail, but a poet too weak to overcome the handicaps of the language" [II:312]. As the indestructible classicist warmed to the defense of French rhyme, he compared its use in tragedy to the presence of color in a painting.

The primacy of the lines of poetry over the action of the drama Voltaire upheld even in the second portion of his dramatic production, during the period when spectacle was most frequently utilized. In the "Epître dédicatoire" to *Tancrède,* Voltaire declared that a sublime thought and emotion were more important than any amount of pomp and apparatus on the stage. The ability to evoke the sublimity and effectiveness of thoughts and feelings depended, of course, upon the artistry of the poet to overcome the restrictions imposed by language and rules. When Voltaire relied upon dramatic staging and the histrionic talents of skilled performers, he sincerely felt that he was merely supplementing the beauty and power of the poetic lines; he always condemned spectacle for spectacle's sake. At the time of *Sémiramis,* in a discussion of tragedies and operas, his derogation of extravaganzas for the eye contained this comment: "Those people do not know that four lines of beautiful poetry are worth more in a play than a whole regiment of cavalry" [IV:500]. That this was his consistent view is adequately shown by his use of almost the identical words nearly twenty years later in the Preface to *Les Scythes:*

> It is a hundred times better to give actors good lines than to preoccupy oneself with their actions. We can not repeat too often that four lines of beautiful poetry filled with feeling are worth more than forty postures on the stage. Woe unto the person who seeks to please by pantomime, solecisms, and bad verses that are an insult to the language [VI:269].

Most of the sweeping condemnations of Voltaire's poetry could well be the result of a sort of reflex action. The traditional notion that his poetry is worthless has become so deeply ingrained over the years that it is amusing to see the maneuvers consciously or subconsciously resorted to by some critics who, although unconvinced of its unworthiness, have yet not succeeded in liberating themselves from the tyranny of tradition. Raymond Naves, finding laudable qualities in *Mérope,* felt constrained to say: *"Mérope,* which has long remained a classic for its edifying theme, is an estimable play, renewing without too much unevenness the central subject of *Andromaque."* [31] A few pages later the double negative was again pressed into service to perform the delicate task of praising the lyricism of Voltaire— equivalent, in a sense, to praising Satan at a religious gathering. Following the customary pattern, Naves first condemned him categorically: "Voltaire as a lyrical poet is nonexistent." Then càme the usual qualifier, praise negatively affirmed: "This does not mean that he lacked lyrical verve, or more exactly an elegiac gift; he paraphrased 'The Song of Songs' and especially the 'Ecclesiastes' into verse which is not insignificant." Even this dubious approval seemed inappropriate for a writer universally condemned as a bad poet; a tried-and-true formula is then employed to set the scales in proper balance: "But he is not capable of sustained lyricism; he cannot let himself go. The moral concern and more precisely his didactic nature leads him back to prose or the familiar type of poetry." [32]

A more recent critic follows a different yet equally familiar approach. Voltaire is condemned for not having filled the poetic void of the eighteenth century. This sin of omission became one of commission: "one suspects Voltaire of having failed because of his own fault"; [33] in other words, he did not properly and capably utilize his talents. After all, did not Diderot describe Voltaire as an "excellent specimen of poetic organization"? In short, he is accused of having treacherously permitted the authentic poetic flame to become extinguished between Racine and Chénier. (From this type of criticism, and incidentally it is very common, Chénier always gains what Voltaire loses.) An important reason for Voltaire's failure, it is argued, was the absence of the built-in critic who is indispensable to every great classicist; this prevented him from overcoming, as Racine had, the difficulties of the alexandrine line. On the contrary, the evidence seems to prove that he was a better critic of himself and his work than his contemporaries were. For example, the fulsome flattery of rulers and literary luminaries never convinced Voltaire that he was the equal of Racine and Corneille, as many sincerely felt he was. Not that he was unaware of his own genius; humility was never one of Voltaire's virtues. Being cognizant of his own poetic abilities, he would not have accepted with equanimity the statement that he knew that his poems were weak and could do nothing about it. An attempt to corroborate this assertion was made by referring to André Delattre's hypothesis that Voltaire had started *La Pucelle* as a serious work to compensate for the insufficiencies of *La Henriade,* the implication being that he set out to move the mountain, and all that emerged was the proverbial mouse, in the form of *La Pucelle:* a frivolous, vulgar, and irreverent work.

A more rational position was taken by John Morley:

> When people whose taste has been trained in the traditions of romantic and naturalistic art, or even not trained at all except in indolence and presumption, yawn over the French alexandrines [of Voltaire], let them remember that Goethe at any rate thought it worthwhile to translate *Mahomet* and *Tancrède.*[34]

One might add that Schiller also admired *Mahomet* and *Tancrède,* Matthew Arnold considered Voltaire a poet and a good one, Gibbon found *Tancrède* splendid, and Schlegel had general praise for all of Voltaire's theater. Needless to say, no discriminating critic after the eighteenth century has attempted to compare Voltaire with the great dramatists of any country, let alone Shakespeare, Corneille, or Racine. Quite justly, critics find Voltaire's lines somewhat thin, by contrast with the masculine energy and richness of Corneille, and lacking in the perfection and harmony, not to mention the depth and psychological insight, of Racine. When he is compared with the immortal Bard, he falls considerably behind in range, depth, and sheer power. Ironically, many of Voltaire's deficiencies in dramatic verse resulted precisely from that fatal excess of facility that deprives it of the impression of strength. Some of the weakness of his lines stemmed from the greater freedom he sought in versification, in order not to shackle his thought.

Contrary to general belief, Voltaire worked and reworked his material assiduously without necessarily correcting the defects that resulted from his facility, for he was wont to rewrite lines or whole sections instead of polishing the original verses. As a result, any version, whether the first or the fifth, could easily have been dashed off in a matter of days, once the subject was well outlined in his mind. He finished *Olympie* in six days, thereby providing occasion for the witticism that he should not have rested on the seventh. Notwithstanding his vanity and self-assurance, Voltaire further weakened his plays by consulting too many friends, most of whom were not qualified to give professional advice and could at best indicate the average spectator's reaction. What is worse, he too often listened to their suggestions. By contrast, the more systematic Racine had only two or three close advisers to whom he turned for criticism. Another unfortunate habit of Voltaire was that of composing different works simultaneously. At one point he was writing three plays: *Zulime, Mérope,* and *Mahomet.* The last two were virtually written simultaneously, a unique instance in literary creation, since both are works of first rank.

That many of Voltaire's plays have serious flaws is not surprising, when one recalls that he wrote fifty-two plays and that they constitute a small part of his over-all literary production. So prodigious was that literary output that he expressed doubts in a letter to Cramer in 1771 that he would ever successfully negotiate the treacherous voyage to posterity, though it is safe to surmise that he felt his chances of reaching that destination to be better than those of J. B. Rousseau's "Ode à la Postérité" ("Ode to Posterity"). Moreover, in order to gain a truly accurate perspective, all his literary activity should be placed within the larger framework of the innumerable projects that simultaneously occupied his attention. It is a miracle that some tragedies—*Zaïre, Adélaïde, Alzire, Mérope, Mahomet,* and *Sémiramis*—are as good as they are.

The most important factor in Voltaire's incapacities as a dramatic poet was his insistence on the superiority of the epic style and his conviction that the salvation of the French theater lay in the preservation of that style. In spite of his keen sensitivity to the desires and demands of theater audiences, he failed to see that the second half of the eighteenth century had irrevocably repudiated this style and preferred something more natural. Grimm and Diderot, along with La Motte, Marmontel, Mercier, and Beaumarchais, saw clearly that the elevated style of epic poetry in tragedy had outlived its day. Grimm often criticized this aspect of Voltaire's work, though he still recognized him as "the master of all of us." The evidence is clear that Voltaire did not always support his classical ideals in practice, no doubt in deference to the increasing weight of critical opposition. It is equally manifest from his correspondence that when he aspired to the highest levels of artistic and stylistic perfection, he reverted to the "strong" and elevated style. Furthermore, he was personally convinced that his forte lay in this medium, as he explained to his confidant Thieriot: "The epic form is the one I excel in, or I am badly mistaken, and it seems to me much easier to follow a career where one has for rivals Chapelain, Lamotte, and Saint-Didier, instead of trying to equal Racine and Corneille" [Best. 245]. Whatever role one may assign Voltaire in this transitional period of the theater, the popularity of his tragedies over a long interval of time is indisputable. The official booklet published by the archivist-librarian of the Comédie Française shows that from 1680 to 1964 Voltaire ranks eighth in the list of dramatists whose works have been presented more than a thousand times. This fact alone should insure a periodic and unbiased reappraisal of his tragedies. Significantly, as we write these lines, *Orphelin de la Chine* has been revived at the Comédie Française, putting an end to Voltaire's long absence from the historical stage where he, perhaps France's most representative son, so rightfully belongs.

"The height of injustice," expostulated Emmanuel Berl, "was reached when Voltaire, who for over a century incarnated poetry, was branded an anti-poet, an accusation all the more incomprehensible in view of his passion for poetry and the poems he wrote." [35] What modern critics have overlooked in reaching this decision is the chronological, geographical, and linguistic framework within which Voltaire had to work. No writer can be condemned for writing in the manner dictated by his times, nor should that style be judged by the standards of the critic's own time, any more than representational painting can be judged by principles of abstract expression or vice versa. Today, poetry is synonymous with lyrical expression, condensed imagery, obscurity, individually determined license in meter and rhyme, and a wide range of permissibility in the use of words in new contexts. This conception of unfettered creation was not and could not have been that of Voltaire. It is perfectly understandable that posterity's judgment of Voltaire's poetry has been, if anything, more unjust and severe than that of his dramatic works! The verdict is not only subject to the tyranny of opinion working against Voltaire, it has also been based upon an insufficient knowledge of his poems, more so than in the case of his tragedies. Traditional notions have become accepted as facts, and respectability has accrued to these notions through sheer repetition of them. If somehow Voltaire could be granted an additional year of life for every critic who has condemned *La Henriade* as unreadable—without ever having read it—Voltaire would still be here today to defend his own poetry. The least known of his works constantly serves as the focal point of the attacks on his poetry. Yet, when it is seriously examined by Gustave Lanson, the most maligned of Voltaire's works emerges as superior to the "Odes" and is seen as "the highest lesson of the grand classical art interpreted in the delightful style of Louis XV, still theatrical but sprightly." [36]

Today, literary criticism needs some of the daring and irreverence with which Voltaire approached so-called sacrosanct writers. Critics should take to heart the lesson of that delightful chapter in *Candide* where Pococurante refuses to do obeisance to writers of hallowed reputation simply because it is the thing to do. Voltaire's own criticism of such universally acclaimed geniuses as Corneille and Racine—a sacrilege for which some Frenchmen never forgave him—was justified by his intimate knowledge of all their works. Like Pococurante, he refused to render a decision without first having read a work. Too few critics have ever familiarized themselves with a substantial amount of Voltaire's poetry. The selections in anthologies and textbooks systematically exclude Voltaire's more poetic works. Invariably one finds sections of long philosophical poems written in that alexandrine verse that is hardly likely to please the aural and visual senses of the modern reader, a few quatrains as examples of Voltaire's satire and sarcasm, one or two *epîtres* or *stances*, which give the impression they are not supposed to be taken seriously, the usual pages from *La Henriade*, and in the best collections, a passage from "Le Mondain" that does do justice to Voltaire, the poet. On the basis of such a selection, Voltaire's poetic efforts are censured as heavy, monotonous, uninspiring—and unreadable.

There are two well-defined views of Voltaire as a poet. His principal role has been described "as legislator, philosopher, monarch of all the sciences, and a kind of preceptor to the state." [37] Though this function may be a noble and civilized one for a man of letters, the output cannot be expected to qualify as poetry in the eyes of most critics. To this category belong La Henriade and such philosophical poems as "Poème sur la Loi Naturelle" and "Poème sur le désastre de Lisbonne." The other side of this two-faced Janus reveals the disseminator of vitriolic quatrains, leveled at his personal enemies; the poems always cited are those against Fréron and Pompignan. These attack-poems, one must admit, admirably display the ingenious, witty, delightfully cynical, violent, and spiteful Voltaire. The best known are "Les Pour" ("The Fors"), "Les Que" ("The Whiches"), "Les Qui" ("The Whos"), "Les Quoi" ("The Whats"), "Les Oui" ("The Yeses"), and "Les Non" ("The Nos"), directed at Pompignan in retaliation for his disgraceful acceptance speech, delivered before the French Academy in 1760, which had attacked the Encyclopedists in scathing terms. Voltaire's effectiveness with this poetic weapon was undeniable. The poems subjected Pompignan to so much ridicule that he never again during his lifetime dared to appear before the French Academy. Devastating as this type of poetry may be for waging warfare, its poetic quality is less than that of the formal genres that employ the alexandrine lines, so that the constant reference to these quatrains adds nothing to Voltaire's stature as a poet.

Unfortunately, these are the only two facets of Voltaire's poetic output that are generally discussed. Yet there are innumerable poems, seldom read, that belong to neither of these categories and possess poetic merit. If there are those who feel that his long versified compositions are boring and written in a style that lacks movement, color, life—in short, the Voltairean spark—let them read the many epîtres that, "incorporating badinage and satire, are less ponderous than Boileau's and more philosophic than La Fontaine's." [38] Generally, they are written in the eight- or ten-syllable line. Even some epîtres in alexandrine might be perused to advantage, like the "Epître à Horace" ("Epistle to Horace"), written in 1772 when Voltaire was almost an octogenarian. Along with *epîtres* there are the numerous *stances,* which offer many examples of surprisingly sensitive poetry. Among the longer poems, in addition to the well-known "Le Mondain," one should not overlook "Ce qui Plaît aux Dames" ("What Pleases Women"), a whimsical treatment of Dryden's "The Wife of Bath," which in turn was an imitation of a tale by Chaucer that bears the same title.

Detractors and enthusiasts alike are agreed on one point: these less philosophical poems presented in shorter lines and with freer versification are more suitable to Voltaire's temperament and gifts. In the words of someone who is more inclined to question Voltaire's claim to the title of poet than to praise him, "He manifested his sense of rhythm in making an original use of the ten-syllable line." [39] His success in these less learned poetic forms parallels the triumph of the *contes* among the more serious prose works. Freed of the responsibilities and restrictions imposed by the traditional genres, Voltaire's spirit soared free and unrestrained. No longer feeling chained to the inflexible rules of French versification, he abandoned himself to his emotions and used whatever line happened to suit his fancy and purpose. The deeply moving "La Mort de Mademoiselle Lecouvreur, célèbre actrice," though written basically in alexandrine, has interspersed throughout lines of varying length, which change the tempo with dramatic effect. What in less combative hands might have emerged as a typical elegiac poem on the passing of a beloved friend, was transformed by the poet's anger, frustration and sincerity into a challenge hurled at the complacency, bigotry, and stupidity of society. His indignation turned to fury at the thought that many of those who were instrumental in denying the talented artist a decent burial, because her life had not been in accord with some man-made rules of the Church, had been among her ardent admirers when her fame and beauty made her the toast of Paris.

Any number of *epîtres* and *stances* offer quotable lines to demonstrate Voltaire's light, lyrical, and imaginative treatment of subjects more commonly associated with Romantic poets: the themes of love, death, melancholy, and particularly the swift, inexorable flight of time. It is not the author's personal prejudice that motivates so daring a comparison as has been suggested here between Voltaire and the Romantics. True, the critic with preconceived notions, who is intent upon establishing influences and resemblances, can always imagine that he has found valid comparisons between any two writers. Yet, unsympathetic critics of Voltaire's poetry have admitted that many of his lines are so beautiful that they could easily be attributed to such poets as Lamartine, Musset, Vigny, and even Valéry. [40] Voltaire wisely disparaged the translation of poetry by comparing the translation of a poem to a print of a painting. A noted Voltairean pointed out the difficulties entailed in attempting to translate Voltaire's memorable verses:

> They do not admit of translation. It is only in their original tongue that their grace, ease, and delicacy can be appreciated. But for that kind of versifying, they are the model for all time. If Voltaire had not far more splendid titles to fame, he would have gone down the ages as the daintiest and wittiest writer who ever made sonnets on his mistress's eyebrow, trifled with graceful jests, and flattered with daintiest comparisons. [41]

There are many poems better designed to display the poetic gifts of Voltaire. Delightfully saucy is "Epître XLII à Mademoiselle de Guise" ("Epistle XLII to Mademoiselle de Guise"), written in 1734 to the new bride of the Duc de Richelieu, in which he urges her to avenge all the husbands whom her bridegroom has cuckolded by guaranteeing him the same fate. A more typically Voltairean attack, and quite charming, is "La Crépinade," written against J. B. Rousseau, who had become an implacable enemy. Employing his lively wit to perfection in a poem appropriately entitled "La Baronade," he mercilessly satirized Rousseau for having attacked his benefactor, Baron de Breteuil. The "Epître XLVII" of 1733, known as "A Madame la Marquise du Châtelet sur la calomnie" ("To Madame the Marquise du Châtelet, on Calumny"), also has much merit. Especially to be recommended is the reading of two *stances*, one written to his beloved Emilie in 1741, when he was only 47 years of age but already a confirmed valetudinarian, the other written in 1773, near the end of his life. Both poems

possess Romantic qualities one might understandably asso-
ciate with some of the lovely sonnets of Ronsard. Their
themes are the flight of time, the loss of youth, and the sad-
ness and melancholy occasioned by old age. In "Stance XV"
to Emilie he bemoans the denial of physical love brought
about by the debilities of the body. The poet sees two deaths
in everyone's lifetime: the death of the heart, and finally
that of the body. The first, he assures us, is by far the more
painful. Friendship happily arrives to alleviate the pain that
accompanies the first demise. Its beauty and reasonableness
appeal to the mind and compensate for the irreparable loss;
the poet therefore welcomes Friendship. His eyes, however,
are brimming with tears, for his heart still recalls the more
violent and pleasurable delights of the flesh he has been
forced to forsake. No subject could be more typical of
Ronsard, Lamartine, or Musset, and it is difficult to imagine a more lyrical and delicate treatment.

The second "Stance XXXIV," which also contains nine
stanzas, was dedicated to Mme. Lullin. It too expressed regret at the encroachment of old age. At the age of eighty,
however, his memories had been dimmed by time and the
preoccupation with one's infirmities; consequently, the feeling of deprivation was no longer acute. An appreciation of
the compensations that were available in old age made easier the philosophic resignation to one's fate. Snatches of
summer greenery could be discerned under the wintry glaze
of senescence, although their duration was all too short.
The tone of the poem is sad; it stresses the divorce from
meaningful life as one becomes increasingly concerned with
the problems of aging, and ends on a metaphysical note
of enquiry reminiscent of *Le Philosophe ignorant*. The
poem that best portrays the poet as he contemplates the rav-
ages of time, deplores the inability of the body to match
one's desires, and bemoans the swift passage of man's al-
lotted time on earth, is the "Stance L" entitled "Les Désagré-
ments de la vieillesse" ("The Unpleasantnesses of Old
Age"). As Voltaire surrendered to the movement of the
poem rather than confine himself to the rigid alexandrine,
he sprinkled octosyllabic lines liberally throughout the
poem. Another evidence of his sense of freedom is his abandonment in the last three stanzas of the pattern that he used

in the first three. The result is a spontaneous and natural quality otherwise impossible to achieve; the last stanza particularly illustrates the effect that is gained by changing the line. For those convinced that Voltaire's poetry is devoid of lyrical qualities, we recommend his translation of "The Song of Songs." He selected this section of the Bible because it was in his estimation so tender and beautiful, qualities he was quite capable of appreciating—and expressing—in French.

The bulk of Voltaire's poetry unquestionably does not possess either the evocative and suggestive power that transcends the surface meaning of the words or the lyrical flights of pure beauty so frequently sought in poetry. For the greater part of his poetic production, Richard Aldington's description is on the whole an accurate one:

> The virtues of Voltaire's verse are in the main virtues of good prose; facility, smoothness, clarity, evenness of tone, epigrammatic felicity, good sense, invention. It is deficient in imagination, passion, the sense of mystery, vivid metaphors and images, a plastic sense.[42]

He does nevertheless take the precaution to precede the above definition with these words: "Matthew Arnold thought him a poet, a great poet. Any work that Matthew Arnold has praised must be treated seriously and with respect."

Probably the finest single poetic effort of Voltaire is *La Pucelle*. Written in epic form so as to ridicule Chapelain's conservative and exalted treatment of Joan of Arc, it was consciously patterned on Ariosto's *Orlando Furioso*. Voltaire greatly admired the Italian epic poet, and his admiration became adulation later in life when an increased knowledge of Italian permitted him to savor fully the delicacy and charm of *Orlando Furioso*. "Ariosto is my God; all poems bore me but his," he wrote Mme. du Deffand in 1761 [Best. 8772]. There is no doubt that Voltaire never considered *La Pucelle* a serious epic, as André Delattre conjectured, but a work of fantasy and badinage, pure burlesque for entertainment and release-of-pressure value during his periods of more serious composition. The cantos were composed at irregular intervals over a span of some thirty years, most of them undoubtedly during the Cirey years, for a constant concern of Emilie was how to keep this explosive work under lock and key in order to prevent its unauthorized dissemination.

The work is admittedly vulgar and grotesque from a strictly moral and religious point of view. In particular, the twenty-first canto, the original "donkey canto" that describes the submission of Joan to the wily devil-inspired wooing of the donkey, surpasses Rabelais in coarseness, though the excellence of the burlesque is without parallel. In all probability, Voltaire was simply giving open expression to the marked penchant for pornography, common in many men, to compensate for their own body's increasing impotence. The spirit of the time permitted such license. Indeed, during Voltaire's lifetime, *La Pucelle* enjoyed a popularity rarely accorded any other literary work of its day. "Nowhere," Henri Blaze deBury tells us, "is Voltaire more Voltairean than in *La Pucelle*." And some pages later he added: "All over Europe they spoke only of this masterpiece. In France, it was Richelieu's breviary; in Berlin, the Queen Mother implored the author to grant her readings of the work, to which the Princess Wilhelmina listened from behind the tapestry." [43]

La Pucelle does not equal the *Orlando Furioso* for sheer poetry, yet it is unquestionably a poetic delight. Natural squeamishness, personal insecurities, or inner guilt often restrain the average reader from exploring the charm of this burlesque masterpiece, in which Voltaire's great range of poetic skills enjoy full sway. Rarely can one find more delicate irony, more beautifully turned verses, more appealing and captivating passages of lyrical quality. Unhappily, too many of those who do read it find themselves incapable of surmounting moral, religious, and nationalist barriers; they cannot therefore abandon themselves to the indisputable enticements and pleasures of this poem, so masterfully rendered in decasyllabic verse. *La Pucelle* is the answer to critics who insist that Voltaire was incapable of a sustained work of real poetic merit. All that is required for a full appreciation of its literary delights is a temporary suspension of one's moral judgment and a willingness to approach this burlesque epic with an open mind. Despite its licentiousness, the Voltaire who emerges is the familiar humanist, whose altar was humanity and whose high priest was reason.

Most of Voltaire's poems are vehicles for his philosophic ideas; a great many of his long poems, it is true, have the added disadvantage of having been written in the heavy-footed alexandrine that is capable of stifling all save very talented poets. In advocating a reappraisal of Voltaire's poetry, then, no one presumes to claim for Voltaire the rank of a major lyrical poet. On the other hand, to deny him any stature as a poet is an injustice of comparable gravity. The prevailing judgment is unduly influenced by a limited acquaintance with the poetry and by present standards that are conceivably subject to change. Our contention is that if readers of Voltaire will peruse many of the countless poems that are now seldom read, the result will be added delight at the discovery of heretofore unsuspected gifts. Whether a more favorable re-evaluation of Voltaire's poetry will follow is really immaterial. Voltaire, who had greater faith in posterity than he professed, will continue to survive those who repeatedly consign him to oblivion. His survival is assured by the fact that his poetry is so vital to his theater, and plays so important a role in the expression of his philosophical ideas.

CHAPTER V

∽❀∽

VOLTAIRE,

PHILOSOPHER

OF HUMAN PROGRESS

*W*hether one considers Voltaire, as Macaulay did, "the king of wits and the God of fools," or concurs with Brunetière that both "Voltaire and Jean-Jacques Rousseau had so many grave blemishes of character that we are tempted when we think of the one always to prefer the other," no one challenges the pre-eminence of Voltaire's role as a humanist and humanitarian. Certainly few writers have been more concerned with man's effort to achieve liberty and peace. The charge may be made that his efforts were more practical than theoretical and that his campaigns, however commendable, were directed to putting out flash fires instead of attacking problems at a broader or deeper level. Critics also quarrel over the constructive or destructive nature of his work. One thing friend and foe agree upon is that "the spirit of gentle humaneness runs . . . through his life: a love for humanity, unprincipled if you like to call it such, because he saw human values that transcended all abstract notions and moral absolutes." [1]

The human progress advocated by Voltaire took many

forms: material, intellectual, social, and ethical. His defense of luxury was dictated by an appreciation of its role as an agent of progress. The author of "Le Mondain" was not merely expressing a sybaritic desire for physical comforts or a dilettante preference for intellectual pleasures. The voluptuary yielded to the hard-headed realist, who recognized the value of a prosperous economy and a flourishing commerce for the eradication of most of man's troubles. Luxury, instead of being the nefarious manifestation of a corrupt society that it was for Jean-Jacques Rousseau, became a worthy stimulus to greater achievements, which would prove beneficial both to the individual and the nation. That is why he praised unreservedly the conditions in England, where commerce was pursued by noble and bourgeois alike, whereas in France the nobility scorned the *commerçant*. The essential and indispensable role of commerce was expounded in "Sur le Commerce," the tenth letter of the *Lettres philosophiques*.

At the intellectual level, Voltaire set an admirable example. All knowledge, not excluding the sciences, fell within the scope of his intellectual curiosity. He frequently satirized medicine, precisely because it did not keep abreast of the latest scientific discoveries. In the eleventh letter of the *Lettres philosophiques* he deplored the backwardness of France in treating smallpox. By comparison, England and many other countries were more advanced, more open to accepting the fruits of progress. Unfortunately, the stupidity of the doctors was aided and abetted by the unenlightened attitude of the state, and particularly by the Church. Voltaire, who had almost died of smallpox in 1723, had a very personal reason for resenting the interference of the Church with scientific advance.

At times Voltaire despaired when he was confronted with the unconscionable negligence on the part of the "leaders" in France toward keeping pace with scientific progress in all fields. In *Traité sur la tolérance* he exclaimed:

Will we always be the last to embrace the constructive views of other nations? They have moved forward. When will we? It took us sixty years to adopt the principles of Newton; we have scarcely begun to save the lives of our children through inoculation; only recently have we begun to rely on the more modern techniques of agriculture. When will we begin to practice the true principles of humanity? [XXV:59].

In England, Voltaire contended, both eyes had been open for over a hundred years. "The French are beginning to open one eye, and there are persons who would not permit us to become one-eyed" [XIX:576]. Peace, liberty, and prosperity—those magic goals of mankind—were impossible without the advancement that comes from learning and scientific discoveries. He therefore consistently supported and praised the undertaking of the *Encyclopédie*, because it represented a giant step in the right direction. His own contribution consisted of forty-three articles, the first three articles of which appeared in Volume V at the end of 1754.

Ethics always received his greatest attention, because of its supreme importance for man. Without satisfactory and salutary relationships among men, social intercourse deteriorated and all forms of progress were endangered. The *Lettres philosophiques* (1734), characterized by Gustave Lanson as "the first bomb against the Ancien Régime," represented a milestone in the struggle to liberate man from the political and religious shackles of the past. True, the germinal essence of the same ideas as those propounded in the *Lettres* can be found in most of Voltaire's preceding works. But in no previous work do the essentials of militant Voltaireanism emerge so forcefully. In this work he took up the cudgels for humanity with more serious intent, as indicated by his comment in the famous "Remarques sur les Pensées de Pascal" ("Comments on the Thoughts of Pascal") that generally constitute the twenty-fifth letter: "I dare come to the defense of humanity against that sublime misanthrope" [XXII:28]. In this same letter he prophetically charted the course he was to follow: "Man is born for action, as fire is destined to rise and a rock to fall" [XXII:41]. All of Voltaire's subsequent works were to breathe that same spirit and determination that characterize the man of action. In the serious philosophical poems, in particular the "Poeme sur la Loi Naturelle," which was in all likelihood composed in 1752 for the edification of Frederick II, the message of Voltaire was tolerance and justice.

The world had witnessed too much evil, injustice, intolerance, and outright persecution because of the narrow prejudices and blind superstition of limited and unreasoning minds. Voltaire's unrelenting war against religion sought to undo the harm it had brought upon society through the puppet-like manipulation of unthinking persons. "Superstition is to religion what astrology is to astronomy, the very mad daughter of a very wise mother," Voltaire warned. "These two daughters have long held the earth in subjugation" [XXV:100]. Two things had to be accomplished to undo the harm: (1) man had to become enlightened enough to see the shortsightedness of his own selfishness and greed, which had produced barbarous customs, political injustice, and discrimination; (2) the power of religion to corrupt men's minds and to inflict harm had to be curtailed. Because he realized that the first would necessarily be a long and involved process, he concentrated his attacks on religion, while at the same time trying in his own inimitable way to promote the education of the masses. The "Prière à Dieu" ("Prayer to God") in "Traité sur la tolérance" is a model of deistic submission to God; in it we find the constantly recurring theme of Voltaire's message:

I no longer address myself to man, but to You, eternal God of all beings and of all worlds. If feeble creatures lost in the immensity of the universe can dare question You who have given all and whose decrees are immutable and eternal, deign to take pity on the mistakes that stem from our human nature and prevent our errors from bringing about our suffering and destruction. You have not given us a heart to hate each other, nor hands to strangle one another. Make it possible for us to help each other to support the burden of a painful and ephemeral life. May You prevent our different clothes, insufficient languages, ridiculous customs, imperfect laws and foolish opinions from becoming causes for hatred and persecution. Let those who light candles in broad daylight in Your honor cherish those who content themselves with the light of the sun. Prevent those who clothe themselves in white garments to worship You from detesting those who dress in black. Make it permissible to honor You in either an ancient tongue or a new one; and oh

Lord, make those who possess land or rounded fragments of metal called money be less proud of their riches and position. And may the poor look upon the rich without envy, for You know that wealth and titles are unworthy reasons for vanity and pride.

Have all men remember that they are brothers! Implant in their hearts the same horror of tyranny exerted on the soul of man that they have for the theft by force of the fruits of their work and peaceful industry! If the plague of war is inevitable, let us not hate one another and torture each other in times of peace. And let us employ the short period of our existence in thanking You, wherever we may reside, be it in Siam or California, and in whatever language we command, for the life You have granted us [XXV: 107–8].

Voltaire's unforgettable campaigns to seek redress in individual cases of injustice have been seized upon, curiously enough as proof that he was more inclined to concern himself with isolated instances than with political systems of grand and theoretical design, such as those one associates with Montesquieu and Jean-Jacques Rousseau. The need for the grand design is unquestionable. But can one really discount the emotional impact of a highly dramatized case of flagrant injustice? It is precisely the inflammatory nature of the specific example that fires men's minds into action. The emotionally charged works of Jean-Jacques Rousseau may have offered more terse aphorisms to inflame the minds of such revolutionaries as Robespierre and Saint-Just, but the works of Voltaire certainly did more than simply prepare the minds of men for the acceptance of change. When Voltaire was emotionally greeted in 1778 upon his return to Paris after twenty-eight years of absence from the capital, the masses were acclaiming the passionate defender of the downtrodden, not the political, sociological, or philosophical theorist. He rightfully belongs in the forefront of the group of writers whom Bernardin de Saint-Pierre had in mind when he exclaimed: "It seems to me that some favorable revolution is in store for us. If it comes, it will be letters that we will have to thank for it. . . . Oh men of letters! . . . You alone recall the rights of man and of the

Divinity." [2] In truth, the crowds surging around Voltaire in 1778 were a prefiguration of what was to occur eleven years later.

No greater distortion of Voltaire's thought and action is imaginable than to believe with Emile Faguet that he was never concerned with the rights of man and consequently contributed little if anything to the Revolution or to the spirit of the Revolution. Only Mme. de Stael's remark that the author of *Candide* revealed an insensitivity to human misery and suffering could be further from the mark. Her criticism in *De l'Allemagne* (*On Germany*) reads in part:

> He had a singular antipathy for final causes, optimism, free will, in short all the philosophical opinions which uphold the dignity of man. He wrote *Candide*, a work of infernal gaiety. It seems to have been written by a person with a nature different from ours, a person indifferent to our fate, happy with man's suffering, and laughing like a demon or like a monkey at the misery of the human race with which he has nothing in common. [3]

Forgetting for the moment all question of degree of influence or importance either in his own time or on posterity, can one seriously contend that Montesquieu, Diderot, or Rousseau—to mention the three other great names of the eighteenth century—loved man and mankind more than Voltaire? By comparison with him, Montesquieu and Rousseau were as withdrawn from the social stream as monks. Diderot too was far less directly involved with his fellowmen, in spite of his tremendous labors on the *Encyclopédie*. The misfortunes of man, individually or as a social unit, affected Voltaire physiologically, viscerally. It is difficult to imagine any one of the three writers mentioned above developing a fever on every anniversary of the massacre of St. Bartholomew, as Voltaire reportedly did. "Oppressed innocence melts my heart; persecution makes me wild and indignant," he wrote the Comtesse de Lutzelbourg on September 2, 1753 [Best. 4855]. Thirteen years later, his reaction to the torture and execution of the Chevalier de La Barre proved the sincerity of those words. The incident provoked the following outburst in a letter to d'Argental, July 16, 1766:

The atrocity of this deed seizes me with horror and anger. I am sorry that I have ruined myself in buildings and improvements on the border of a country where, in cold blood, and on the way to dine, barbarities are committed which would make drunken savages tremble with horror. And that's what you call a gentle, light, and gay people! Cannibalistic harlequins! [Best. 12537].

It is true, as Renée Waldinger concludes, "that Voltaire never foresaw the Revolution and the changes it was to effect, that he never thought of a revolution as a means for achieving his goal, and that he did not even anticipate the end of the Old Regime." [4] Following her example, one should not attach too much significance to the often-quoted comment made by Voltaire in a letter of April 2, 1764 to the Ambassador Bernard Louis Chauvelin: "All that I see adds to the seeds of a revolution that seems inevitable, and which I shall not have the pleasure of witnessing" [Best. 10968]. Like Montesquieu and most of the *philosophes*, Voltaire was a realist who recognized the inevitability of gradualness in the correction of existing abuses. He never advocated the abolition or serious curtailment of the monarchy. Yet, without realizing it, he made an inestimable contribution to the advent of the Revolution and to the eventual triumph of republicanism by undermining the previously sacrosanct position of the monarch. What is more, he did more than anyone else to weaken religion, the staunch ally of the monarchy. Through his efforts, the people became conditioned to the idea that a king *can* do wrong; acceptance of this idea facilitated the recognition of the wrong that did exist. The subjects of the king were finally awakened to the realization that, however menial their position, they possessed both natural and civil rights. The gradual erosion of the power that religion exercised over the minds of men in turn brought about a shift in outlook: the people no longer tended to look to heaven for their rewards. More and more they sought them on earth in their own immediate social surroundings, thereby providing a fertile ground for political and social upheaval.

At the first stages of political uprising, the imprint of Voltaire's ideas was quite marked. Many of the abuses detailed in the "Cahiers" ("Notebooks") that were drawn up in 1789 by the three orders for the Convocation of Estates had on numerous occasions been grievously attacked by Voltaire. It is noteworthy that the grievances presented in these official "Cahiers" held out the hope that solutions could be found through reformation of the monarchical system. In other words, as late as 1789, the very year of the Revolution, an enlightened monarch who would be more attentive to the needs of his subjects was seen to be still capable of correcting those very abuses that had at last produced this overwhelming disenchantment and dissatisfaction with the status quo.

Voltaire is commonly accused of having been merely a popularizer and generalizer of others' ideas. Without doubt, he did not ascend into the rarefied atmosphere of the frontiers of philosophical thought; he may even have been incapable of such solo flights, because his realistically oriented mind would accept only the demonstrable and measurable results of sense perceptions. Nevertheless, as René Pomeau has pointed out, if one reads Voltaire carefully and with an open mind, "one will have to admit that the great metaphysical problems intrigued and disturbed him all his life, not just occasionally." [5] For the forging of systems he had only scorn: such efforts to transcend the limits of human experience inevitably produced, in his opinion, facile and ingenious explications that were completely meaningless and useless to man.

By temperament Voltaire resisted any reasoning that was not anchored in a reality capable of being verified by the senses. In the exordium to "Poème sur la Loi Naturelle" he admonished philosophers, metaphysicians, and theologians, whom he compared to blindfolded gladiators:

> Let us abandon these fantasies called systems
> And to progress let us study human nature [IX:442].

The infallible guide had to be reason, tempered and supported by past experience. The pure Cartesian reason of the speculative rationalist was unacceptable to eighteenth-century utilitarians, for whom theories had to be buttressed by the ever-growing stock of psychological and scientific data. Cognizant though he was of the advances made in these areas, Voltaire adamantly held that "We are all still as ignorant of first principles as we were at birth" [XXVI:49]. No one remained more convinced of this than Voltaire, yet no one worried the subject more, if the number of times he introduced references to such speculation is any reliable criterion. As late as 1773, in his lyrical *stance* to Mme. Lullin, he ended the poem with a speculation on death and the afterlife [VIII:540].

Despite the uncertainties inherent in metaphysical speculation, Voltaire did not advocate that it be abandoned. The exploration of the transcendent or the supersensible intrigued him as forcefully as he rejected it. The theories of fundamental causes, the nature of matter, the conditions of knowledge, and the perennial problem of good and evil were assiduously investigated by Voltaire. Even when he was reasonably certain that the human mind could never ascertain the answers, he could not prevent himself from asking questions, for his doubts and interrogations enabled him to avoid all the pitfalls that one could encounter in so difficult a field of inquiry as metaphysics. The more obscure and abstruse the problem, the more he insisted upon clarity of presentation, so great was his distrust of the mental gymnastics and verbal obfuscations of most philosophers, which contributed nothing to human advancement, as he saw it, and should therefore be condemned. He severely censured those who in his estimation were capable of making worthwhile contributions if only they would turn their thoughts to more useful pursuits. On the other hand, philosophical speculation by such great minds as Hobbes, Locke, Descartes, Bayle, and Condillac could serve a purpose, without their necessarily always being right. When he believed a definite benefit could be derived from such studies, he actively encouraged them. For example, he urged Condillac in 1756 to establish himself at Ferney, in order to incorporate in one magnum opus all the philosophical ideas from his three works: *Essai sur l'origine des connaissances* (*Essay on the Origin of Knowledge,* 1746); *Traité des sensations* (*Treatise on Sensations,* 1754); and *Traité des animaux* (*Treatise on Animals,* 1755).

The potential danger from investigations by inferior minds was all the more evident to Voltaire when he saw the confusion that the half-dozen superior minds of men such as Descartes, Malebranche, and Berkeley were able to produce, as they grappled with problems that Voltaire felt would always remain beyond the ken of man's finite intelligence. For, as he explained to Frederick in a letter of April 25, 1737: "Metaphysics is made up of two components, as I see it: first, that which all men of reason know; second, what they will never know" [Best. 1260]. Carried away by the passion of his convictions, the incurable utilitarian sporadically pushed a relatively acceptable argument as far as the rejection of all metaphysical inquiry, a position that has been rendered absurd by modern standards, as well as by Voltaire's own investigations: "And when I suppose they have spoken in an intelligible manner, what good will come of it? We have already established that the things understood by so few persons are useless to the rest of mankind" [XXVI:61]. In Voltaire's defense one might note that, even after two hundred years of incredible advances in man's knowledge, many of the things he refused to accept as truths—such as the immortality of the soul and the divinity of Christ—still remain as unverifiable today as they were in the eighteenth century.

Voltaire was interested in philosophy and the sciences both as a humanist, within whose province all knowledge fell, and as a humanitarian who appreciated the inescapable impact of ideas upon society. The latter invariably triumphed over the former, or as one Italian critic phrased it: "For Voltaire the fundamental problem remains the Baconian accord and union of knowledge and method, and the interpretation of nature with practical applications uppermost in mind." [6] It would be wrong to conclude from this realistic and utilitarian preoccupation that Voltaire stressed the practical to the exclusion of the theoretical. He himself made this abundantly clear:

> I am far from implying that one must limit oneself blindly to what is practical, but it would be desirable indeed for physicists and geometers to make a real effort to fuse practicality with speculation [XXII:186].

His vanity notwithstanding, Voltaire never included himself among the select group worthy of profitably undertaking these inquiries. This explains the references to his speculations as mere amusements. One of the most fruitful and interesting "amusements" for an appreciation of Voltaire's interest in metaphysics is the "Traité de Métaphysique," composed during 1734 for the moral and spiritual instruction of Emilie, and never published during his lifetime. In the treatise he soberly studied the fundamental questions that have always preoccupied the philosophers and metaphysicians: the origin of man, the immortality of the soul, the existence of God, and the essence of matter. Quite often in this treatise he presents the arguments of others, only to refute them through analogous reasoning—one of Voltaire's favorite methods of argumentation. In a letter of June 27, 1734 to Formont he explained the origin of the work: "I reread Locke. I dared to amuse myself by following his method of reasoning. I wanted to comprehend my existence and to see if I could not establish certain basic principles" [Best. 741]. The insistence that these works were only diversions should not mislead the reader into underestimating either their seriousness or their value. Chapter VII, "Si l'homme est libre" ("If Man is Free"), is among the more lucid discussions of this thorny subject.

Like most of the *philosophes,* Voltaire believed in a deterministic philosophy. The problem for him was to establish the essential freedom of man within the deterministic framework. Resorting to analogy, he gives the example of a man who acts erratically, driven by circumstances that exist at a particular moment of decision. The observer might be tempted to infer that this was proof that such a man was not the master of the situation, never was, and never could be. According to Voltaire's pragmatic and sensible approach to problems, that type of reasoning resembles this:

> Men are sometimes sick, therefore they are never well. Now who can not see the impertinence of this conclusion? Who can not see that, on the contrary, to be aware of illness is irrefutable proof that one must have enjoyed health, and that to feel one's enslavement and impotence to act proves that one previously possessed the power and liberty of choice? [XXII:218].

In a discussion of liberty in *Le Philosophe ignorant,* he argued that his conception of man's freedom of action did not contradict his support of determinism, which granted the individual varying measures of freedom to shape the conditions that would exist at any given point of decision and thereby determine man's choice: "What I have said is that man's liberty consists in his ability to act, not in the chimerical 'Will to Will' " [XXVI:93]. With his penchant for reducing everything to practical levels, he scornfully insisted that "when one says that man is not free to will, this does not affect in the slightest man's liberty, for liberty consists in acting or not acting, not in willing or not willing" [XXXIV:328]. He stated his position even more directly in the section "De la Liberté" of the *Dictionnaire philosophique*: "Your will is not free, but your actions are. You are free to act when you have the power to act" [XIX:582].

There can be little doubt that this was fundamentally Voltaire's view on the question of liberty. When terribly depressed by the world and man's miserable condition, he could, as he did in a letter to Frederick II, January 26, 1749, express a different opinion: "I wanted so much for man to be free, and I have done all in my power to believe it. Experience and reason convince me nonetheless that we are machines destined to function for a certain length of time in accordance with the Will of God" [Best. 3349]. However, readers and critics alike should be chary of extracting isolated views from a correspondence as voluminous as that of Voltaire and accepting them as significant contradictions of formally stated positions. One should always keep in mind that ideas expressed in letters often reflect passing moods, or may be deliberately aimed at accomplishing a specific purpose, relevant to the circumstances of the letter. Moreover, Voltaire is a mine of contradictions, as are all exceedingly prolific writers, expecially since, as in the case of Voltaire, he "opposed the relative to the absolute and substituted the critical approach for the dogmatic in all the domains of philosophy." [7] One of his grievances against Descartes was that he spoke with such a positive tone on such speculative subjects as *tourbillons* and elements. What made this all the more condemnable was Descartes' pretension that his philosophy was based on systematic doubt. Voltaire himself admitted to little certainty in the philosophically important *Dialogues entre A,B,C*

(*Dialogues Between A,B and C*) [XXVII:398]. In spite of these protestations, he enjoyed an incontestable advantage over the more theoretical philosophers: his ideas could be tested against human experience, that is, in the ever-present laboratory of society.

Because of the importance of the principle of man's freedom in the development of a sound ethic, Voltaire directly refuted the materialists' arguments against the existence of God. The gift of choice was supposedly God-given. Consequently, the elimination of God, he feared, might deprive the average man of the consciousness of choice in action, and society as a viable structure would thereupon disintegrate. In Voltaire's eyes, therefore, there could be no profitable discussion on the question of whether God exists, for a negative answer was inconceivable. Whether fired by intellectual or humanistic convictions, he always embodied logic and clarity in the methods he employed to combat the various theories he disagreed with. Unfortunately, Voltaire instinctively slanted any discussion of hypotheses he considered to be socially detrimental, in order to justify his preconceived notions. This preoccupation with the utilitarian aspects of any philosophy sometimes proved to be his Achilles' heel, for he was too prone to dismiss any argument that seemed to oppose the public interest, regardless of its intrinsic merits. This insistence on utility was symptomatic of the age. One indication is the anecdote related by Mme. de Graffigny, author of the *Lettres péruviennes* (*Peruvian Letters*), who spent much time at Cirey and recounted the happenings there. She recalls that one evening an English scientist-geometrician spent much time laboriously calculating the probable size of the inhabitants of Jupiter. In describing the reaction of the group, she said: "We were highly diverted by the folly of an intelligent man who would spend so much time and effort on a thing so useless." [8]

Even as a generalizer of others' ideas, Voltaire never accepted an idea without first having studied it carefully. As a result, he rejected the ideas of men whom he admired greatly, and at the same time admired ideas propounded by others with whom he disagreed violently. For example, he applauded Plato's conception of God as "the eternal geometer," endowed with a creative intelligence. By the same token, however, he deplored Descartes' abandonment of his great genius as a geometer and mathematician in the formulation of his philosophical ideas, because in doing so he had succeeded only in substituting a new chaos for that of Aristotle. Leibnitz he favored over Newton for his interchangeability of elements, and he encouraged everyone to read Spinoza, finding his acceptance of a central intelligence praiseworthy. On several occasions, he did not hesitate to attack even the great Locke when the latter strayed into theological speculation, though on the whole he vigorously applauded the practicality of Bacon, Locke, and Newton. The truth is that Voltaire always attacked any ideas that he felt led only to confusion and thereby further complicated the efforts of persons like himself, who were trying to reduce physical and metaphysical knowledge to a workable system of ethics.

Voltaire's rejection of philosophical and metaphysical theorizing was threefold: (1) the limitations of man's mind rendered much of this theorizing fruitless; (2) the failure to follow the Baconian inductive method led to untenable conclusions; (3) there was little inclination to place philosophy in a setting of human experience. The last was undoubtedly, in Voltaire's eyes, the gravest sin for "that which is not universally useful, not comprehensible to the average man and unintelligible even to the cultivated minds, can not be necessary to humanity" [XXVI:70]. Thus the works of a Descartes or a Spinoza were ineffective in influencing the man on the street. "Why? Because man's conduct is determined by custom and not by metaphysics. A single eloquent and able man can do much to influence mankind; a hundred philosophers can accomplish nothing if they are only philosophers" [XXVI:69]. Indeed, the figments of their fertile imaginations might do much harm if they were accepted as truths.

It was as the eloquent and skillful transmitter of ideas and illuminator of recondite questions that Voltaire saw his own role. The measure of his success can best be suggested by the comments attributed to Mme. de Choiseul and Empress Eugénie. The former said of him: "What is it to me that he tells me nothing new, if he develops what I have thought, and if he tells me better than anyone else what others have already said? I do not need to have him teach me more than anyone else knows, and what author can tell me so passing well as he what everyone knows?" [9] The Empress Eugénie betrayed the average human being's partiality for the mystery of things when she said: "Voltaire . . . I shall never forgive him for having made me understand things which I shall never understand." [10] And Condorcet, an eminent disciple of Voltaire, gave this opinion of him: "Voltaire's life ought to be the history of progress that the arts owe to his genius and the power he exerted on the opinions of his century—in short, of the long war he waged against prejudices, a war declared in his youth and maintained to his dying day." [11]

Some critics, confusing manner with matter, have accused Voltaire of superficiality. To be sure, the light touch of the master ironist and satirist, which often descends to sarcasm and burlesque, is misleading. Many find it disconcerting to have serious subjects expounded in lucid prose and treated in a light manner; they prefer ponderous and abstruse phraseology, as though profundity of thought can or should be equated with unreadability or unintelligibility. Voltaire was adamantly opposed to jargon; he wrote in a light, piquant style that was as much a part of him as his thoughts. An example of the irrepressible imp in Voltaire emerges in his discussion of liberty: "To be truly free is to be physically able to do something. When I can do what I wish, that represents liberty for me. My liberty, in short, consists in walking when I wish to walk and do not have the gout" [XXVI:56].

But does the ingredient of laughter really vitiate or impede thought? Does the ironic presentation of "André Destouches à Siam" ("André Destouches in Siam," 1766), published as a Supplement to Le Philosophe ignorant, detract from the forcefulness of Voltaire's condemnation of the barbarous customs still prevalent in his day: rampant venality, glaring injustices stemming from the unequal and haphazard application of a multiplicity of laws, the use of torture, and the inequitable assessment of taxes? Surely Croutef's description of the conditions in France could only produce sober reflection and indignation, just as the smiles provoked by *Zadig* and *Candide* vanish when the full force of Voltaire's criticism is skillfully driven home. Alberto Cento warns against our being deluded by the facile and only apparent superficiality of Voltaire's method and manner: "In reality his comments contain the entire program of a new humanism." [12]

A charge often made against Voltaire is that he possessed insufficient knowledge of the subjects he treated. Fernand Vial avers: "One can be virtually certain that, with the exception of Locke, he never read in their entirety and methodically the great philosophical works. His ideas were hastily acquired and he gives the impression of having scanned all of Plato in one afternoon." [13] To substantiate this contention we are given a garbled version of Gustave Desnoiresterres' story of André Deluc's visit to Ferney in May 1755 in the company of M. de Beaumont, during the course of which Deluc tried unsuccessfully to engage Voltaire in a discussion of Condillac's *Traité des sensations*. Suspecting from Voltaire's embarrassment that he had not read it, Deluc dropped the subject. To his amazement, a few hours later, once Voltaire presumably had had the opportunity to read it, he discoursed on it brilliantly enough to elicit Deluc's applause. To begin with, the property of Ferney was purchased in 1758. Moreover, Deluc's letter to Tremblay clearly states twice that only "quelques momens" had elapsed. Furthermore, M. de Beaumont later told Deluc that he had discussed the book with Voltaire after Deluc's vain attempt to engage Voltaire in an exchange of views and that Voltaire had undoubtedly merely repeated his (Beaumont's) ideas. What is more important, Desnoiresterres expressed his doubts as to the veracity of the whole story, and argued that if it were true (and one must remember that Deluc was a friend of Jean-Jacques Rousseau), "What the anecdote really proves is Voltaire's marvelous powers of assimilation." [14] Similar charges by other critics are no more tenable upon closer inspection.

Wagnière assures us that Voltaire had a prodigious memory, and the size of Voltaire's library still provides the most eloquent testimony of the scope of his intellectual curiosity and the breadth of his reading. It contains, Professors Havens and Torrey reveal in their carefully prepared *Vol-*

taire's Catalogue of his library at Ferney, 7,500 volumes and between 2,500 and 3,000 titles.[15] The important role that books played in his life was best expressed by Voltaire himself in various comments scattered throughout his correspondence. Two of them read: "If I do not have books to read, I become very unhappy" [Best. 3857]; and "I carry books with me when I travel, just as heroines of novels take diamonds" [Best. 4828]. To be sure, no one can deny that Voltaire was a fast, perhaps sometimes too fast, reader. Anyone who reads as much as he did must of necessity sin in this respect. But to brand his over-all work as the superficial result of inadequate and faulty preparation, one must overlook the tremendous erudition and the encyclopedic learning that were embodied in such masterpieces as the *Dictionnaire philosophique* and the *Essai sur les moeurs*.

It is ironic, in view of his sense of mission, that Voltaire has emerged as a negative and destructive figure. There would be as much validity in describing the work of a surgeon as being destructive or the preachings of Jesus Christ as too general. In fairness to these critics, it should be admitted that the form and style of the philosophical tales and of the light verse do permit this impression, for in these he was primarily, although by no means exclusively, on the attack and therefore more destructive than constructive. In addition, the literary forms of these works precluded a systematic presentation of either abuses or reforms, not to mention the fact that Voltaire was by temperament opposed to methodical works that were capable of boring the reader. Nor did he want to prejudice his propaganda effort. But, as Jane Ceitac has wisely noted, "his destruction itself, in holding up a new ideal, encouraged the creation of something new."[16] The fact usually overlooked is that Voltaire did write many other works not as well known as his *contes*, in which he catalogued, more scrupulously and effectively than he had in the *Lettres philosophiques*, the evils stemming from the tyranny and bondage of the Church and state. Among these are: "Traité de métaphysique," "Traité sur la tolérance," *Dictionnaire philosophique*, "Commentaire sur le livre des délits et des peines" ("Commentary on the Book of Crimes and Punishments"), *Essai sur les moeurs*, and "Prix de la justice et de l'humanité" ("Reward for Justice and Humanity"). The recommendations in some of these works were often presented in pages of outline form—such as to delight even the filing-cabinet type of mind.

Some eighteenth-century critics also accused Voltaire of not being constructive enough in his approach. The defense he offered appears in the conclusion of "Examen de Milord Bolingbroke," written around 1736 but not published until 1767. After laboriously cataloguing the evils of Christian fanaticism, Voltaire maintained that any man of reason should on the basis of the evidence hold Christianity in horror and adopt the simple religion of Theism (or Deism), under which man would adore God and love his fellowman. Instinctively realizing that man, who needed something more definite to cling to, would challenge the seeming vacuum that he created by his rejection of all the trappings of established religion, he posed the inevitable question:

> What shall we put in its place, you ask? What? A ferocious animal is destroying my neighbors; I tell you to get rid of that beast, and you ask me with what we shall replace it! . . . My answer is: God, truth, virtue, laws, punishments, and rewards. Preach probity and not dogma. Be priests of God and not of man [XXVI:299].

The defense itself has been judged to be imprecise, and strictly speaking it was. Voltaire assumed—and rightly so, to judge from the results of his writings—, that an attack upon an abuse implied the needed correction. When, for example, he attacked the stupidities of doctors, the recommendation was obvious—they ought to keep abreast of the advancements of medical science. When he decried the iniquitous disparities in the laws of France, the greater advantages of uniform laws were manifest. Similarly, the exposure of the ludicrousness of tariffs or taxes between provinces left no doubt that their elimination would benefit commerce. The list is endless.

Voltaire was striving for the creation of an atmosphere of tolerance, in which the Bastille would no longer be the answer to every honest doubt and objection. He sought to create a moral climate that was based on human values. Once this had been achieved, the new moral outlook would lead to the passage of better legislation, and serve as a major determinant of men's actions until the desired legislation could be realized.

The two ingredients necessary to effect this revolution of the mind, thought Voltaire, were truth and reason. With them the ignorance and credulity of the masses could be vanquished, and man's supine posture before Church authority brought to an end. Absolutely essential to the accomplishment of this peaceful revolution were "enlightened and magnanimous ministers, wise and humane prelates, and a ruler who knew that his own interest and glory depended upon the happiness and flourishing numbers of his subjects" [XXV:37]. The task was difficult and required endless effort, too much for any one man, however skillful and dedicated he might be. For assistance, Voltaire turned to his fellow *philosophes*, those noble souls who could serve ideally as examples to the masses. He urged them incessantly to forsake their less useful tasks and to dedicate themselves to this crusade.

Contrary to the consensus of most critics, Voltaire recognized the advisability of proceeding gradually in the correction of existing abuses. In all likelihood, it was this concept of moderation that determined his acceptance of the usefulness of a punishing and rewarding Creator, a divinely endowed freedom of will, limited to be sure to "the power of action," and a Natural Law, "the only law that a God who was the Father of all human beings could have given them" [I:240]. Equally evident to Voltaire were the advantages of effecting the desired political and legislative changes within the framework of the existing monarchical structure. In a word, despite the uncompromising tactics employed during the Calas, Sirven, Chevalier de La Barre, and Montbailli campaigns, Voltaire's over-all strategy underlined the necessity of first, with the aid of speech and pen, establishing a greater harmony between man's thoughts and his actions, in conformity with his true nature. At the end of "Traité sur la tolérance" he described the role he hoped his own works would play in this long struggle: "I sow a grain that one day will be able to produce a harvest" [XXV:114]. The same strategy underlay his opposition to the Church. He recognized the danger of abruptly overthrowing Christianity. Instead, he placed his faith in the future enlightenment and conversion of the average man into a responsible citizen [see XXVI:299–300].

When Voltaire referred to citizens, he was not thinking of flag-waving patriots, but rather of individuals who placed the Golden Rule above racism and chauvinism. As much callousness and oppression could result from unchecked and unreasoning "patriotism" as from his dreaded foe, organized religion, for he knew all too well that all one needed to do was beat on the skin of an ass with two sticks to inflame men's minds to irrational acts that were devoid of any semblance of humanity. "The civic fibre vibrates in Rousseau, that which vibrates in Voltaire is the universal fibre. One can say that, in the fruitful eighteenth century, Rousseau represented the people; Voltaire, still more vast, represented Man." Elsewhere in the same eulogy, delivered at the centenary commemoration of Voltaire's death, Victor Hugo paid him the supreme compliment: "Let us say it with a sentiment of profound respect: Jesus wept; Voltaire smiled. Of that divine tear and of that human smile is composed the sweetness of the present civilization." [17] For Voltaire, moral and political progress had to be social. With Alexander Pope he believed: "That reason, passion, answer one great aim/ That true self love and social be the same." [18] The subordination of self to society depended primarily upon the enlightenment of the monarch, and secondarily upon a citizenry that was rescued from the clutches of a repressive religion and made cognizant of their rights and duties. Until the people were able to rely upon restraints developed through reason, the moral safeguards contained in religion should be retained.

In practice, to be sure, the excitable Voltaire often lost sight of his theories. When a particularly shocking crime was committed against humanity, he willingly risked both the security and the comforts of his worldly surroundings in the hope of redressing a glaring injustice. At such times, the "consummate craftsman in the art of making ideas effective in the lives of men" [19] wielded his satirical scalpel with unparalleled efficiency, as he ruthlessly exposed the incredible abuses, injustices, and intolerance that infested France. Nowhere did he catalogue and document these evils as thoroughly as he did in the *Dictionnaire philosophique* and the *Essai sur les moeurs*. These works reveal a man who was motivated by a noble sense of duty and obligation to the human race. Grimm attributed these qualities to Voltaire in his review of *Essai sur les moeurs*:

> All his writings radiate a love for virtue and a generous passion for the welfare of humanity, and there is no work in which this is more evident than in the universal history. It would be difficult to have too low an opinion of a people who, constantly exposed to such works, failed to become more civilized, enlightened and just.[20]

Admittedly, the constructive elements in this monumental history are not presented in a readily accessible manner; they are dispersed throughout a mass of material. The format of the *Dictionnaire philosophique* permitted the presentation of the same abuses and recommendations in a more systematic way. This massive three-volume work, written in the same serious tone as the *Essai sur les moeurs*, is perhaps the most important single repository of Voltaire's suggested reforms. In the article "Gouvernement" ("Government"), written in a style reminiscent of the *Lettres persanes*, a supposed stranger is describing the conditions he has encountered during his travels in 1769 [XXIX:287–91]. Among the most objectionable evils pointed out are those repeatedly scored by Voltaire: the lack of uniformity of laws; the unfair tax structure; the venality rampant in judicial, military, and civil positions; the corrupt financial structure; the absurd duties levied within France itself. By way of contrast, one section examined conditions past and present in England, summarized the rights and privileges of the English citizen before the law, and forthrightly advocated patterning French laws upon those of England [XIX:296–97]. He later made a similar study of English laws in his "Commentaire sur le livre des délits et des peines," and again observed that, in France, "Wherever one looks, one finds contradictions, inflexibility, uncertainty and arbitrariness. In this century, we wish to perfect everything; let us try then to perfect our laws, upon which our lives and fortunes depend" [XXX:577].

All forms of injustice grieved and infuriated Voltaire; the most deplorable were those that had been created by the very laws that in theory should have had as their goal the elimination of injustice. For that reason he warmly welcomed the Marquis de Beccaria's *Traité des délits et des peines* (*Treatise on Crimes and Punishments*), translated into French in 1766 by the Abbé Morellet. "By his great contribution to the new atmosphere of enlightenment Voltaire had helped to prepare a favorable ground for reforms. Without this preparation Beccaria's treatise could hardly have appeared, and criminal reforms . . . would probably have been indefinitely postponed." [21] In turn, Beccaria's book helped to systematize Voltaire's ideas. The influence is especially noticeable in "Relation de la mort du chevalier de La Barre" ("Account of the death of the Chevalier of La Barre," 1766) and "Commentaire sur le livre des délits et des peines" (1766), both of which made strong pleas to make the punishment fit the crime, in conformance with the recommendations listed in Beccaria's treatise. Indisputably, these works of Voltaire contributed vitally to preparing French minds for a speedier acceptance and incorporation of Beccaria's reforms.

Voltaire's continuing interest in the legislative and judicial systems was demonstrated in his "Prix de la justice et de l'humanité," written at the age of eighty-two. A contest had been announced and a prize of fifty louis offered for the best essay on criminal legislation. That this interested Voltaire goes without saying. After doubling the prize by a personal contribution, he proceeded to write on the subject himself in order, as he explained, to offer future competitors "our doubts on this important subject, so that they may resolve them if they judge them worthy" [XXX:534]. Despite his conservative tendencies in some areas, Voltaire foresaw grave danger in protracted delays in revising the judicial and legislative systems. Failure to do so might conceivably lead to violent expressions of dissatisfaction by the people. In the "Traité sur la tolérance" he invited "those who are at the head of governments and those destined for high office" [XXV:31] to examine carefully the benefits that they themselves would reap from a system of laws grounded on human rights and human values.

There was never any doubt in Voltaire's mind about the desirability of establishing the supremacy of the state over the Church: "Make all the members of the clergy subject to the government, because they too are subjects of the state" [XIX:625]. Ideally, the clergy should accept this voluntarily; if necessary, however, it should be imposed upon them, since the authority of the Church "is and can only be spiritual . . . it should enjoy no temporal power" [XVIII:432]. Nor should the Church continue to superintend general education; Voltaire saw that instead as the proper function of the state. In brief, the Church had to relinquish to the state any control over men's external actions and confine its activities exclusively to the spiritual relations between man and God.

One of the most forceful sections of the *Dictionnaire philosophique* is "Les pourquoi" ("The Whys"). These are grave questions, designed to make the reader pause and reflect on the conditions prevailing in the eighteenth century. Absent is the usual Voltairean mockery, raillery, and persiflage as he ranges in subject matter from the purely utilitarian to the metaphysical. No doubt, some critics would insist that these are still no more than questions. Yet never did he more successfully fulfill his function as "the cutting edge which laid open society to a deeper probing by other minds." [22]

Voltaire often used the dialectical method in the *Dictionnaire philosophique* as a way to convey his ideas. A typical example is the "Catéchisme chinois" ("Chinese Catechism") containing six *conversations* between Cu-Su, a disciple of Confucius, and Prince Kou. Cu-Su, presenting Voltaire's views, tries to counsel the prince, just as Voltaire in real life tried to influence the conduct of many rulers, notably Frederick II. By the sixth *conversation*, Voltaire had his imaginary prince, who had learned his lessons better than the real princes in Voltaire's life, reduce Cu-Su's teachings to two guiding principles for his reign. He told his mentor: "Love of my fellow man will be my virtue on the throne, and love of God, my religion" [XVIII:77]. This was the simple message Voltaire wished to impart to king, legislator, judge, priest, and subject alike. With this lesson learned and practiced, the individual would be free and happy, within a desirable if not an ideal society.

Voltaire's message in behalf of justice, enlightenment, and the over-all triumph of reason can be found in virtually any of his works. The philosophical tales derive much of their value from their "fund of philosophy scattered everywhere." [23] Even *La Pucelle*, the burlesque that was meant primarily to entertain his intimate friends, contains a clearcut message to humanity in the "Arguments" that precede each canto. The "Argument" of the fourth canto is typical:

> Si j'étais roi, je voudrais être juste,
> Dans le repos maintenir mes sujets,
> Et tous les jours de mon empire auguste
> Seraient marqués par de nouveaux bienfaits,
> Que si j'étais contrôleur des finances,
> Je donnerais à quelques beaux esprits,
> Par-ci, par-là, de bonnes ordonnances;
> Car, après tout, leur travail vaut son prix.
> Que si j'étais archevêque à Paris,
> Je tâcherais avec le moliniste
> D'apprivoiser le rude janséniste [IX:75].

In essence, he would be just and benevolent if he were king; generous, if in charge of finances; and cooperative and fraternal, if archbishop of Paris. It is significant that even in so frivolous a work as this, Voltaire could not resist the opportunity to make his usual strong plea for the brotherhood of man based on mutual respect, love, and assistance. And the plea as usual was especially directed at those in positions of power, since their virtuous actions could naturally be expected to have greater immediate effects, in addition to lasting and long-range influence. Voltaire, like Confucius, had a simple if not actually oversimplified theory of government: if the ruler is upright, the people will imitate him.

The "Avis au public sur les parricides imputés aux Calas et aux Sirven" ("Advice to the Public on the Parricides Attributed to Calas and Sirven," 1766) was inspired by Voltaire's desire to present the case for humanity, once he had been struck by the "degree to which both these incidents were intimately linked to the general welfare of the human race. "We thought," he added, "that it would be in the interest of mankind to attack at its source the religious fanaticism that produced them" [XXV:520]. Conditions had happily improved, and no one was more aware of this than Voltaire. Still, "the germ subsists," he warned. "If you do not stifle it, it will spread over the earth" [XXV:531]. Should reason fail to assert itself, whatever the risks, the same horrors that had plagued the past would recur. Voltaire's self-assigned task was to expose at every opportunity conditions that needed correction, sometimes employing mockery, irony, and satire, as in the philosophical tales or in poems like "Le Mondain," at other times the more sober tone of "Poème sur la Loi Naturelle," "Poème sur le désastre de Lisbonne," "Traité sur la tolérance," "Traité de métaphysique," and Le Philosophe ignorant. And as we have seen, he could, when he was so inclined, resort to the almost irresponsible burlesque and buffoonery of La Pucelle or to the more vindictive style of "La guerre civile de Genève" ("The Geneva Civil War"). Whatever the form, whether poetic, narrative, dramatic, epic, epistolary or historical, and regardless of the motivation—sometimes it was not the most noble, as in his Sentiment des citoyens— there always emerged a defense of man's natural rights to liberty and happiness.

With regard to general education for the masses and man's rightful role in the government, an undue emphasis has been placed on some random comments that were made by Voltaire in his correspondence. True, in a letter to Collini of July 31, 1775, he seemed to be accepting a system of second-class citizenship when he reasoned that property owners, being more responsible, should have more voice in the government. But the pragmatist was simply reflecting the conditions of the time. The realities of the situation called for such temporary solutions; the revolutionary leaders themselves recognized this, to judge from the limitations they imposed on the right to vote. It would be wrong to conclude that either Voltaire or the revolutionary leaders saw this as the ideal long range goal for the population. The "canaille," as Voltaire called the laborers when he was irked by their behavior, were in fact enormously ignorant, and the educational program that was carried on under ecclesiastical direction was for the most part inadequate and inappropriate. Being a realist, he regretfully recognized the unlikelihood of improvements in the near future.

When the rich, conservative landlord momentarily predominated over the humanist-humanitarian, or when he was particularly exasperated by the stupidity and folly of the masses, Voltaire could even become convinced of the uselessness of trying to educate the *manouvriers* at all. After all, he would reason, "the working man does not read; he works six days a week, and on the seventh goes to the cabaret" [XVII:2]. Therefore, it was the bourgeois—the ones most likely to profit from an education—who should be instructed. Despite these understandable outbursts, which his natural goodness and generosity made him regret when they were brought to his attention, Voltaire realized that only education, on as broad a scale as conditions permitted, would eventually break the spell of religious fanaticism and lead to the passage of laws that were capable of guaranteeing man's rights and of promoting the arts and commerce, thereby eventually insuring peace. The naturally optimistic nature of Voltaire enabled him to believe in the perfectibility of man, an indispensable requirement to project the intimately linked goals of a workable ethic and happiness.

The greatest threat to man and progress, naturally, was war. France had unfortunately suffered many senseless and useless wars that had devastated the countryside, decimated the population, and bankrupted the nation. What was even worse, from the point of view of civilization and human progress, was the fact that the arts had been stifled. Voltaire's prescription for the average man's happiness and for social harmony may have been the "cultivation of one's garden" as expressed in *Candide*. His personal "garden," his own way of life, required the intellectual and sensual pleasures supplied by the arts. The arts for Voltaire were not the overrefinements of an effete society as they seemed to Jean-Jacques Rousseau, in whom Voltaire saw a dangerous enemy of progress; they contributed immeasurably to the enlightenment of man, and he saw a direct correlation between the degree of enlightenment and that of morality, just as there was between morality and man's happiness. To demonstrate the efficacy of the arts when they were all directed toward a useful goal, he pointed to St. Petersburg where wonders had been performed. "The emulation of the arts," he exulted, "has changed the face of the earth from the foot of the Pyrenees to the snows of Archangel, the Russian seaport on the White Sea" [XVII:432].

If the great achievement of the eighteenth century was indeed "to have raised questions of fundamental importance which until then had been hushed up, to suggest lines of inquiry," then Voltaire played a leading role "in making the connection between philosophy proper and actual problems, in asking 'How?' and 'To what good?' and so contributing on the highest plane to an improvement in the art of living." [24] Voltaire, the humanitarian "citizen" of the world, strove ceaselessly to establish the "natural" and inalienable prerogatives of man: "liberty of person and property, trial by due process of the law, freedom of speech and assembly, liberty to worship God as dictated by the individual conscience, and the equal right of all human beings to pursue their happiness or self-interest." [25] The two obstacles to the accomplishment of these goals were the Church and the state. The power of the former to disseminate intolerance eventually had to be crushed, for Voltaire feared that it would always oppose change. The latter, the liberal monarchist hoped, could be reached with an educational program carried on by all the *philosophes* and designed to highlight the injustice of many laws and practices.

Neither age nor an increasing tendency toward pessimism succeeded in curtailing Voltaire's efforts to "propagate learning, encourage the arts, commerce, industry, and to develop tolerance, respect for liberty, and love of progress." [26] As we have noted, with the events of the late fifties and early sixties, Voltaire's righteous wrath was inflamed to a new pitch. His actions and theories were completely fused, and he became the veritable conscience of mankind. The sustained cry of protest that emanated from Ferney did not, however, constitute a parenthesis in Voltaire's life, as was the case with Zola's "J'accuse" ("I Accuse") defense of Dreyfus. It is wrong, therefore, to assume from Voltaire's intensified tactics, as André Delattre did, that with the exception of some possible indication in the *Lettres philosophiques*, there was no evidence before 1760 of Voltaire the reformer and defender of the oppressed.[27] The fight Voltaire waged during the Ferney period was the same one he had carried on at a more theoretical level throughout his life. He had only shifted into the high gear of the journalist and polemicist. In a real sense, the aroused humanitarian tended to suppress the literary man, but what the world may have lost in literature it certainly gained in the progress of human rights, which literally and figuratively made it possible for man to cultivate his "garden" in greater peace and tranquility.

With the emergence of philosophy in the nineteenth century as a separate discipline, which stressed primarily questions that were insoluble by empirical or formal methods, Voltaire's reputation as a philosopher has gone into gradual eclipse. It has become unfashionable for philosophers to dedicate themselves to the practical aspects of philosophical inquiry. In eighteenth-century France, on the other hand, the identification of philosophy with science— which, by twentieth-century standards, had vitiated philosophical thought—produced the *philosophes* or natural philosophers, who were on the whole more interested in human progress than in the progress of the human mind. And Voltaire was by popular consent the leader of this group, the one who had unquestionably contributed the most in the struggle to make man a happier and freer member of society. Yet, ironically, despite a lifelong effort in behalf of humanity, it is Voltaire's reputation as a destructive thinker that has steadily grown. Critics have classified him pejoratively as a "practical" rather than a "real" philosopher. Typical of this criticism of Voltaire is Macaulay's statement: "Voltaire could not build; he could only pull down; he was the very Vitruvius of ruin. He has bequeathed to us not a single doctrine to be called by his name, not a single addition to the stock of our positive knowledge." [28]

To be sure, in the narrow and formal sense of the nineteenth and twentieth centuries, Voltaire was not a philosopher. He was not primarily interested in the general principles, theories, or laws that regulate the universe and underlie all knowledge and reality. Nevertheless, he was a lover of wisdom and truth, vitally interested in the processes that govern thought and conduct; etymologically, it is certain, these fall within the purview of philosophy. The fact that he never formulated systems should not in itself exclude him from the ranks of philosophers. D'Holbach was no more original than Voltaire, for example, and he is frequently included in formal courses of philosophy. The *Système de la nature* (*System of Nature*), d'Holbach's best claim to admittance into the ranks of formal philosophers, is unquestionably a broader and more systematic treatment of the many problems that preoccupied the attention of most of the *philosophes*. Voltaire, more than most, examined all these same problems—although, one must admit, in a less methodical, less thorough, and more frivolous manner. Perhaps it was d'Holbach's seeming disinterestedness, his detachment from the arena, that enabled him to gain access to the Olympian spheres of philosophy. Voltaire's personal involvement, on the other hand, his commitment to causes and his sallying into the fray, deprived him of the aura of the thinker. He was too obviously the gladiator, dedicated to such specific goals as the restoration of the dignity of the individual and the alleviation of social ills.

Whether we describe Voltaire as a practical philosopher, a critic of philosophy, a mere popularizer, a sociologist, or a psychologist, the fact remains indisputable that he was a lover of justice and a defender of man. The truth that interested him was the truth that had to do with man and his social existence. He differed sharply from the professional builder of philosophical systems by this constant focus on the human face of philosophy—ethics, the one phase of philosophy with which man was directly concerned in his daily living, and what is more important, the one that could be most useful to man. Two principal interests governed his thought: "a tolerant deism, more moral than theological; an anthropocentric philosophy, searching to organize social life according to terrestrial values." [29] To reach the largest public most effectively, he adopted the combative and destructive stance necessitated by the conditions of the eighteenth century, patterning his style on that of Joseph Addison, the much-admired author of *Cato* (1713), whose goal had been "to enliven morality with wit and temper wit with morality." Nothing more accurately describes Voltaire's treatment of his themes, or better explains why his works enjoyed much greater popularity than did such more exhaustive but pedestrian works as *La Morale universelle* or the *Système de la nature* of d'Holbach.

From unreflective habit, one is often inclined to accept Voltaire's wit as a masquerade for substance. This is to do grave injustice both to one's own powers of discernment and to Voltaire's noble contribution to progress in religious tolerance and civil justice, and his role as promoter-extraordinary of commerce, the arts, and the sciences. All these facets of progress would ultimately lead, Voltaire optimistically believed, to the noblest achievement of human endeavor: Peace—the supreme virtue of civilization, just as war is its greatest crime.

CONCLUSION

$\mathcal{F}$rom the vantage point of the twentieth century, one often feels, on reading Voltaire, that he is unnecessarily "rekilling"—to use the word with which Candide threatened the baron—the monsters that once were a real threat, but have long since been destroyed. Alas, that is not the case. There will always be a need for a figure to enter the lists as the champion of humanity. Mankind is still plagued by social evils today, although fortunately to a lesser degree. One need only recall the concentration camps of World War II, read of man's inhumanity to man for racial and ethnic reasons, or attend a meeting of any committee designated to select potential candidates for political office and see the importance they attach to a possible candidate's national origin and religious faith, to know that Voltaire's fight for tolerance and justice is still necessary in our supposedly enlightened world.

Many persons in the eighteenth century had sincerely come to believe that the evil conditions of the past had been largely corrected. Sometimes Voltaire himself became encouraged enough to be similarly persuaded; then a new outbreak of intolerance would succeed in destroying his peace of mind, sending him hurrying back to his desk to counterattack. The last lines of his *Le Philosophe ignorant* contain this warning to the more complacent souls: "The monster still exists and whoever seeks the truth risks being persecuted. Should one remain idle and turn one's head, or light a torch that will illuminate the way?" Voltaire was incapable of closing his eyes to wrongdoing, no matter what personal inconvenience or sacrifice was involved for him. He was not a professional "do-gooder," impelled to act by an empathic malaise of some sort at the sight of another's suffering. His motivation was primarily intellectual; it was imbedded, nevertheless, in a deep-rooted humanism and humanitarianism. Like many of the world's great crusaders, he was compelled to defend a cause for the sake of the cause itself, regardless of the personalities or persons involved. Voltaire was one of those dedicated fighters for human rights who fortunately do appear in times of need and selflessly march forward to wage the never-ending battle against injustice.

By his own example, Voltaire attempted to arouse others to join him in his crusades. Unlike many misguided visionaries, who stubbornly disregard the facts of life, he was an idealist who was firmly anchored in the realities of the conditions about him. As the battle became more complex in later years, he pursued his ideal concept of society with a logic and realism that would have done justice to a skillful lawyer. The measure to which he succeeded is evidenced by the frequency with which his name is coupled with the emergence of *la mystique républicaine,* although ironically enough he was a confirmed monarchist.

> It is Voltaire and Rousseau, and sometimes Montesquieu and Condorcet, that one finds almost always behind the living influence of France on the masses and ideologies of South America, of the United States itself, of central and eastern Europe and that one will find tomorrow in Africa and Asia.[1]

The "liberal" ideas of the eighteenth century, so staunchly defended by Voltaire, were rooted in an unshakable faith in man and in his ability to better his life on earth. The modern world could with profit learn from Voltaire the necessity of extending one's vision beyond national boundaries. Although he has become identified with France, Voltaire was extraordinarily cosmopolitan and international in outlook, perhaps because he was never blind to the faults of his own country and sincerely believed that a man was a man before he was a Frenchman or a German. In this sense, ironically, he seems to have followed the teachings of Christ more closely than did those who persecuted him for being an Anti-Christ. An even greater irony from a social point of view is the general acceptance today of Jean-Jacques Rousseau as the most modern of the *philosophes;* from a realistic point of view, the latter was so out of step with the future that he discouraged the development of better communication between nations, pessimistically seeing in such progress the seeds of greater evil. Voltaire, by contrast, saw only the promise of better things in any increased intercourse between peoples. He knew that the world of tomorrow could ill afford to remain provincial and narrowly nationalistic—the stakes are too high and the risks too severe.

The greatness of Voltaire lies in the fact that a famous literary figure, important enough to have dominated all the major genres of literature for many generations: history, drama, poetry, *contes,* or epic, should have intentionally devoted so much of his time and energy to the long struggle to improve the conditions of man. The works of other great writers have had deep and lasting effects on the lives of men; Voltaire is among those who consciously and actively joined battle with the forces of injustice, sparing neither money, leisure, time, nor peace of mind.

The place of Voltaire in the literature of France and of the world is beyond dispute. Just as Victor Hugo has become synonymous with French poetry, Voltaire is almost invariably the first to come to mind when one is asked to name a French writer. Understandably, critics will continue to debate his relative merits in any particular genre, or to challenge the reputation he enjoyed in his own day as a dramatist and poet. Perhaps carried away by their own persuasive arguments, some will overlook in the process the fact that Voltaire was the most literary of all the *philosophes*—poet as well as pamphleteer, dramatist as well as historian. By contrast, Montesquieu was principally an historian and Diderot's interests were substantially diverted to scientific investigations and the interminable work on the *Encyclopédie*.

As he himself explained, in a letter to his niece Mme. Denis, his enemies will never succeed in altogether burying him. As long as man cherishes reason, Voltaire, the Apostle of Reason, is assured of immortality, so effective was his use of reason both as an instrument and as a weapon. In addition, the trenchant style of his prose will forever represent the highest expression of incisive wit and clarity. No one has used his mother tongue more efficaciously to give life and meaning to ideas. Each new century may place a different emphasis on the content of Voltaire's works, but the charm and grace of his linguistic presentation will always be indisputable. Keeping in mind Voltaire's advice on the need to adopt an historical perspective, one should not exclude the possibility that future generations may conceivably restore to Voltaire a greater measure of recognition than he now has in the fields of drama and poetry.

Underpinning the undeniable delight of his piquant style are Voltaire's ideas themselves, which help to give his writings a universal appeal that changing times cannot significantly alter. For what Voltaire was incessantly advocating, beyond the elimination of specific abuses, was the necessity for a constant guarding of our thoughts and actions so that human prejudices of whatever kind might never be able to affect adversely the lives of one's fellowmen. He was offering the world "a way of thinking, a method designed to insure the liberty and freedom of humanity by the application of reason. . . . In the twentieth century such an ideal is neither obsolete nor outmoded. Voltaire remains the best master for anyone interested in 'cultivating his garden.' " [2] The underlying premise of the eighteenth century was that human nature always has been and will continue to be the same. If this is true, the same drives will operate in time-tested ways to bring grief and suffering to others—only the forms of injustice and intolerance may vary. Consequently, whatever the social situation of the future may be, and however advanced man becomes through progress in science and technology, the ideas of Voltaire will continue to be applicable.

A recent critic has noted that the three great characteristics of Voltaire's time were "clandestinity, humanism, and the search for new art forms." [3] On the basis of these criteria, Voltaire must emerge as the greatest representative of the eighteenth century in France. He was certainly notorious as a clandestine writer. Some writers, like d'Holbach, were less associated with their work, hidden as they were behind a cloak of almost total anonymity or pseudonymity. But no one resorted to more stratagems, subterfuges and, where necessary, bald lies than did Voltaire. The verbal smoke-screens with which he surrounded each publication must have delighted his own friends, from whom he did not intend to hide his authorship. The case for Voltaire's humanism requires no further defense, if we accept humanism as meaning a way of thought or action that is concerned with the interests and ideals of people. Indeed, the objection of many critics would be that it intruded too much into his writings and detracted from their purely literary value. As for the new art forms, Voltaire not only perfected the philosophical tale, which is associated with his name and has become identified with the eighteenth century, he also modified significantly the format of both drama and historiography.

The eighteenth century is likewise commonly referred to as the Age of Reason or the Age of Enlightenment. Who, more than Voltaire, insisted on the application of reason in every field of human endeavor? His only fault in this respect was his too great insistance upon and faith in pragmatic reasoning processes in such matters as religion and metaphyics, which by their very nature sometimes transcend the perception of the limited senses. It was his confidence that reason would prevail in diplomatic maneuverings, irrespective of national considerations and personal ambitions, that caused his failure whenever he ventured into diplomacy. So great was his faith in reason as the surest path to enlightenment, that every work he wrote, from the shortest love poem to the most massive history, explicitly or implicitly carried the exhortation to ameliorate *la condition humaine* by adopting a more humanistic and truly "Christian" approach to solving the problems that beset social man. In spite of his limited faith in the masses as they were then constituted, "Voltaire never wavered in his conviction that knowledge was superior to ignorance, that enlightenment could never be anything but useful. But he did waver in his estimation of who was ready to absorb enlightenment." [4]

Two defenses of Voltaire admirably sum up his enduring contribution as a writer and humanitarian: those of Diderot and of Fréron *fils*. Diderot, who met Voltaire for the first time upon the latter's return to Paris in 1778, can hardly be accused of being a biased defender of Voltaire. As for Fréron *fils*, it is impossible to imagine anyone who would have had less reason or desire to praise the man who had directed the most vindictive sarcasm against his father. Fréron *fils* published the following assessment of Voltaire's work in the *Orateur du Peuple*:

> . . . he used his great talents to crush superstition and fanaticism, the destruction of which accelerated the birth of our liberty. That is his claim to the eternal gratitude of the friends of the Revolution which his writings prepared! That is why he merits today triumphal honors from a grateful nation! I am perhaps the only person in France who is not a Voltairean, yet the freedom of my country is so precious, so sacred to me, that I can no longer see in the philosopher of Ferney the irascible writer who belched forth invective and calumny, but the great man and benefactor of humanity. [5]

When Naigeon expressed disgust at the shocking behavior of Voltaire, Diderot answered:

> But that madman, as you call him, introduced the philosophy of Locke and Newton into his country, attacked the most sacred prejudices on the stage, preached freedom of thought, inspired tolerance, upheld good taste that was on the wane, performed several commendable actions, and wrote a multitude of excellent works. His name is honored throughout the world and will live forever. [6]

NOTES

CHAPTER I
THE MAN AND HIS BACKGROUND

1. Norman L. Torrey, *The Spirit of Voltaire* (New York: Columbia Univ. Press, 1938), p. 283.
2. Gustave Lanson, *Voltaire* (Paris: Hachette, 1960 ed.), p. 84. The first edition dates back to 1906.
3. Torrey, *op. cit.*, p. 271.
4. George R. Havens, *Voltaire-Candide* (New York: Holt, 1951), p. xv.
5. Emmanuel Berl, *Voltaire-Mélanges* (Paris: Gallimard, 1961, Pléiade III), p. xv of Préface.
6. *Voltaire's Correspondence*, Theodore Besterman, ed. (Geneva, 1953–1965, 102 vols. of text and 5 vols. of index). All future references to Voltaire's correspondence will be to Besterman's edition and will be included in the text; they will be designated by Best. plus the number of the letter.
7. Voltaire, *Oeuvres complètes*, Louis Moland, ed. (52 vols., Paris, 1877–1885). Henceforth, all references to Voltaire's works, with the exception of his correspondence, will be to this edition and wherever feasible will be designated simply by volume and page numbers within the text.
8. John Morley, *Voltaire* (London: Macmillan, 1891), p. 110.
9. Torrey, *op. cit.*, p. 91.
10. *Ibid.*, pp. 177–78.
11. William F. Bottiglia, *Voltaire's Candide: Analysis of a Classic*, in *Studies on Voltaire*, VIIA (Geneva, 1964), p. 297.
12. Paul Valéry, *Voltaire*, Discours prononcé le 10 décembre

1944 en Sorbonne (Collection "Au Voiler" Domat-Montchrestien, Paris, 1945), p. xix.

CHAPTER II

VOLTAIRE'S PHILOSOPHICAL TALES AND STYLE

1. Ira O. Wade, *Voltaire's Micromégas: A Study in the Fusion of Science, Myth and Art* (Princeton: Univ. Press, 1950), p. vi.
2. René Pomeau, *Candide ou l'Optimisme* (Paris: Nizet, 1959), pp. 8–9. Pomeau supports the recent scholarship by Ira O. Wade in his *Voltaire's Micromégas;* it establishes a resemblance between the "Voyages du baron de Gangan" of 1739 and *Micromégas,* and indicates that the *conte* form of fiction had at least been tentatively employed.
3. Norman L. Torrey, *The Spirit of Voltaire* (New York: Columbia Univ. Press, 1938), p. 50.
4. J. H. Brumfitt, *Voltaire l'Ingénu* (Oxford: Blackwell, 1960), p. xlviii.
5. William F. Bottiglia, *Voltaire's Candide: Analysis of a Classic* (Geneva, 1964 in *Studies on Voltaire,* VIIA, 65).
6. Condorcet, "Vie de Voltaire" in *Oeuvres complètes de Voltaire,* I, 241.
7. George R. Havens, *Voltaire-Candide* (New York: Holt, 1951), p. xxix.
8. Bottiglia, *op. cit.,* p. 290.
9. Alexander Pope, *An Essay on Man,* Maynard Mack, ed. (London: Methuen, 1950), p. 51.
10. Bottiglia, *op. cit.,* p. 114.
11. Anatole France, *Le Jardin d'Epicure* (Paris: Calmann-Lévy, 1921), p. 31.
12. Friedrich M. Grimm, *Correspondance littéraire,* Maurice Tourneux, ed. (Paris, 1878), VII, 417.
13. Louis-Mayeul Chaudon, *Nouvelle bibliothèque d'un homme de goût* (Paris, 1777, 4 vols.), IV, 79–80.
14. Brumfitt, *op. cit.,* p. xvii.
15. See Daniel Mornet, *Origines intellectuelles de la Révolution française* (Paris: Colin, 1933), p. 88.
16. Henry N. Brailsford, *Voltaire* (London: Butterworth, 1935), p. 85.

17. John Morley, *Voltaire* (London: Macmillan, 1891), p. 120.
18. Theodore Besterman, *Voltaire's Notebooks* (Geneva, 1952, 2 vols.), I, 26–27.
19. See Gustave Lanson, *L'Art de la prose* (Paris: Librairie des Annales, 1909, 2nd ed.), p. 155.
20. See Bottiglia, *op. cit.*, pp. 258–59.
21. Ruth C. Flowers, *Voltaire's stylistic transformation of Rabelaisian satirical devices* (Washington, 1951), p. 90.
22. André Le Breton, *Le Roman au XVIIIe siècle* (Paris, 1898), p. 215.
23. Brailsford, *op. cit.*, p. 156.
24. This was a variant reading at the head of the XXVth letter "Sur les Pensées de M. Pascal" from the 1739 edition on.
25. Célestin Hippeau, *Le Gouvernement de Normandie au XVIIe et au XVIIIe siècle* (1863–1869) (Caen, 1864), IV, 36.
26. Fernand Vial, *Voltaire, sa vie et son oeuvre* (Paris: Didier, 1953), p. 122.

CHAPTER III

THE HISTORICAL WORKS OF VOLTAIRE

1. See Voltaire's footnote in his *Essai sur les moeurs* (Paris: Garnier, 1963—Classiques Garnier ed.), Avant Propos, I, 196.
2. J. H. Brumfitt, *Voltaire, Historian* (Oxford: Univ. Press, 1958), p. 26.
3. John Bennett Black, *The Art of History* (New York: Crofts, 1926), p. 38.
4. Raymond Naves, *Voltaire* (Paris: Hatier-Boivin, 1962 ed.), p. 116.
5. Gustave Lanson, *Voltaire* (Paris: Hachette, 1960 ed.), p. 113.
6. The three previous quotes come from Voltaire's letter of Oct. 30, 1738 to the Abbé Dubos (Best. 1569). In this letter Voltaire is referring to Isaac de Larrey's *Histoire de la France sous le règne de Louis XIV* (Rotterdam, 1718, 4 vols.; Amsterdam, 1724,

9 vols.); Henri-Philippe de Limiers' *Histoire du règne de Louis XIV* (Amsterdam, 1717, 7 vols.; Amsterdam, 1718, 10 vols.); Guillaume de Lamberty's *Mémoires pour servir à l'histoire du XVIIIe siècle* (La Haye, 1724–1740, 14 vols.); and the laborious compilations of Jean Rousset de Missy, such as his *Histoire du cardinal Alberoni* (La Haye, 1719).

7. Peter Gay, "Voltaire's *Idées républicaines*" in *Studies on Voltaire* (Geneva, 1958), VI, 72.

8. J. H. Brumfitt, Introduction to critical edition of Voltaire, *La Philosophie de l'histoire*, in *Studies on Voltaire* (Geneva, 1963), XXVIII, 11.

9. René Pomeau, Introduction to Voltaire's *Essai sur les moeurs*, *op. cit.*, p. xxiv.

10. *Ibid.*, p. xxv.

11. André Bellessort, *Essai sur Voltaire* (Paris: Perrin, 1950), p. 205.

12. Emmanuel Berl, *Voltaire, Mélanges* (Paris: Gallimard, 1961–Pléiade ed.), Introduction, p. xxix.

13. Norman L. Torrey, *The Spirit of Voltaire* (New York: Columbia Univ. Press, 1938), p. 268.

14. Lanson, *op. cit.*, p. 131.

CHAPTER IV

THE DRAMATIST AND POET

1. Edmond Lefèbvre, "Le Style des tragédies de Voltaire," *Revue Latine* (1905), IV, 444.

2. Ferdinand Brunetière, *Etudes sur le XVIIIe siècle* (Paris: Hachette, 1911), p. 63.

3. Trusten W. Russell, *Voltaire, Dryden and Heroic Tragedy* (New York: Columbia Univ. Press, 1946), p. 2.

4. André Delattre, *Voltaire, l'Impétueux* (Paris: Mercure de France, 1957), p. 92.

5. René Pomeau, *Voltaire par lui-même* (Paris: Editions du Seuil, 1955), p. 58.

6. André Rousseau, *Voltaire—La Mort de César* (Paris, 1964), p. 7.

7. See F. Brunetière, *Histoire de la littérature française classique* (Paris: Ch. Delagrave, 1913), III, 146.

8. Paul Valéry, *Voltaire*, Discours prononcé le 10 décembre 1944 en Sorbonne (Collection "Au Voilier" Domat-Montchrestien, Paris, 1945), pp. xvi–xvii.

9. Russell, *op. cit.*, p. 2.

10. Gustave Lanson, *Voltaire* (Paris: Hachette, 1960 ed.), p. 96.

11. *Ibid.*, p. 97.

12. See Kenneth N. McKee's article "Voltaire's *Brutus* during the French Revolution," *MLN* (1941), LVI, 100–6, for a careful analysis of its popularity. McKee's conclusion: *Brutus* was scarcely more popular during the Revolution than it ever had been, except for a flurry of interest in 1790 that misled Raymond Oxley Rockwood to exclaim in *The Cult of Voltaire to 1791* (Chicago, 1935): "Late in 1790 what good patriot had not attended a performance of *Brutus* or had not heard it quoted, almost as a good Christian might quote Scriptures, as an unanswerable argument on critical occasions" (p. 143).

13. Ronald S. Ridgway, *La Propagande philosophique dans les tragédies de Voltaire* (Geneva, 1961), *Studies on Voltaire*, XV, 240.

14. Max Aghion, *Le Théâtre à Paris au XVIIIe siècle* (Paris: Librairie de France, 1926), p. 416.

15. See Friedrich M. Grimm, *Correspondance littéraire*, Maurice Tourneux, ed., (Paris, 1878), janv. 1774, X, 340–41.

16. See Henri Lion, *Les Tragédies de Voltaire* (Paris: Hachette, 1895), p. 159.

17. Russell, *op. cit.*, p. 141.

18. See Lanson, *op. cit.*, p. 104.

19. See John Morley, *Voltaire* (London: Macmillan, 1891), p. 127.

20. See Ridgway, *op. cit.*, p. 231.

21. Norman L. Torrey, *The Spirit of Voltaire* (New York: Columbia Univ. Press, 1938), p. 88.

22. Robert E. Fitch, *Voltaire's Philosophic Procedure: A Case-Study in the History of Ideas* (Oregon, 1935), p. 17.

23. *Ibid.*, p. 89.

24. Morley, *op. cit.*, pp. 126–27.

25. *Ibid.*, p. 6. See also Voltaire: Preface to *Les Scythes* (VI, 266–67) for his own comments on the subject of originality.

26. Russell, *op. cit.*, p. 9.
27. Lion, *op. cit.*, p. 431.
28. Lanson, *op. cit.*, p. 105.
29. Alexis Piton, "Les Origines du mélodrame français à la fin du XVIIIe siècle," *Revue d'historie littéraire*, XVIII (1911), p. 256.
30. Raymond Naves, *Voltaire* (Paris: Hatier-Boivin, 1962, 7e ed.), p. 109.
31. *Ibid.*, pp. 107–8.
32. *Ibid.*, pp. 113–14.
33. Pomeau, *op. cit.*, p. 54.
34. Morley, *op. cit.*, p. 134.
35. Emmanuel Berl, *Voltaire—Mélanges* (Paris: Gallimard, 1961, Pléiade ed.), p. xxxi.
36. Lanson, *op. cit.*, p. 90. Perhaps there is some hope yet for *La Henriade*. Theodore Besterman recently notified me that an elaborate edition of *La Henriade* will be published this year by O. R. Taylor in three volumes to be published by the Institut et Musée Voltaire in the *Studies on Voltaire* series.
37. Russell, *op. cit.*, p. 1.
38. Lanson, *op. cit.*, p. 91.
39. Pomeau, *op. cit.*, p. 61.
40. See *ibid.*, p. 61.
41. S. G. Tallentyre, *The Life of Voltaire* (London: Smith, Elder & Co., 1945), p. 142.
42. Richard Aldington, *Voltaire* (London: G. Routledge, 1929, 2nd ed.), p. 138.
43. Henri Blaze de Bury, "Jeanne d'Arc dans la littérature," *Revue des Deux Mondes*, LXIX (15 juin 1885), p. 605.

CHAPTER V

VOLTAIRE, PHILOSOPHER OF HUMAN PROGRESS

1. Norman L. Torrey, *The Spirit of Voltaire* (New York: Columbia Univ. Press, 1938), pp. 35–36.
2. Quoted by André Monglond, *Histoire intérieure du préromantisme français de l'Abbé Prévost à Joubert* (Grenoble: Arthaud, 1929), II, 157.
3. See Louis Moland, ed. *Oeuvres complètes de Voltaire* (52 vols., Paris, 1877–1885), I, xli–xlii.

4. Renée Waldinger, *Voltaire and Reform in the light of the French Revolution* (Geneva: Droz, 1959), p. 104.

5. René Pomeau, *Voltaire par lui-même* (Paris: Editions du Seuil, 1955), p. 51.

6. Cesare Luporini, *Voltaire e le "Lettres philosophiques"* (Florence: Sansoni, 1955), p. 100.

7. Georges Pellissier, *Voltaire, philosophe* (Paris, 1908), p. 304.

8. Mme de Graffigny, *Vie privée de Voltaire et de Mme du Châtelet* (Paris, 1820), p. 56.

9. Romain Rolland, André Maurois, Edouard Herriot (Introd. by Geoffrey Brereton), *French Thought in the Eighteenth Century: Rousseau, Voltaire, Diderot* (London: Cassell, 1953), pp. 144–45.

10. *Ibid.*, pp. 145–46.

11. Condorcet, "Vie de Voltaire," in Moland, ed., *op. cit.*, I, 189.

12. Alberto Cento, *Condorcet e l'idea di progresso* (Florence: Parenti, 1953), p. 72.

13. Fernand Vial, *Voltaire, sa vie et son oeuvre* (Paris: Didier, 1953), p. 352.

14. Gustave Desnoiresterres, *Voltaire et la société au XVIIIe siècle* (Paris: Didier, 1871–1876), VII, 132.

15. See George Havens and Norman L. Torrey, *Voltaire's Catalogue of his library at Ferney* (Geneva, 1959), in *Studies on Voltaire*, IX, 17.

16. Jane Ceitac, *Voltaire et l'affaire des natifs* (Paris: Droz, 1956), p. 12.

17. Victor Hugo, *Le Discours pour Voltaire* (Paris: Calmann-Lévy, 1878), pp. 13 and 15.

18. The end of Epistle IV of *An Essay on Man; The Works of Alexander Pope* (London: John Murray, 1871), II, 456.

19. Robert E. Fitch, *Voltaire's Philosophic Procedure* (Oregon: News-Times Pub. Co., 1935), p. 5.

20. Friedrich M. Grimm, *Correspondance littéraire* (ed. Maurice Tourneux, Paris, 1878), III, 362.

21. Marcello T. Maestro, *Voltaire and Beccaria as Reformers of Criminal Law* (New York: Columbia Univ. Press, 1942), p. 153.

22. Geoffrey Brereton, p. xix of Introd. to Rolland, Maurois, Herriot, *op. cit.*

23. Jean-François de La Harpe, *Lycée ou cours de littérature* (Paris: Didier, 1834), II, 706.

24. Brereton, *op. cit.*, pp. xv–xvi.

25. Constance Rowe, *Voltaire and the State* (New York: Columbia Univ. Press, 1955), p. 178.
26. Raymond Naves, *L'Oeuvre de Voltaire* (Paris: Hachette, 1946), p. 111.
27. See André Delattre, *Voltaire, l'Impétueux* (Paris: Mercure de France, 1957), p. 101.
28. Lord Thomas Babington Macaulay, *Life and Works of Lord Macaulay* (London: Longmans, Green, 1897), VI, 684.
29. Raymond Naves, *Voltaire—Dialogues et Anecdotes philosophiques* (Paris: Garnier, 1940), p. v of Introd.

CONCLUSION

1. Henri Peyre, "The Influence of 18th-century French Ideas on the French Revolution," *Journal of the History of Ideas*, X (1949), 63–87.
2. B. Gilles, *Voltaire, son temps, sa vie, son oeuvre* (Paris: Tournier, 1953), p. 145.
3. See Ira O. Wade, *Voltaire's Micromégas: A Study in the Fusion of Science, Myth and Art* (Princeton: Princeton Univ. Press, 1950), p. viii.
4. Peter Gay, "Voltaire's Idées républicaines," in *Studies on Voltaire* (Geneva, 1958), VI, 101.
5. Fréron fils, *Orateur du Peuple*, Vols. 7–8, no. 2 (July 1791), p. 10.
6. Denis Diderot, letter to Naigeon of 1772, *Oeuvres complètes*, Assézat, Tourneux, eds. (Paris: Garnier, 1875–1877, 20 vols.), XX, 73.

SELECTIVE BIBLIOGRAPHY

BIBLIOGRAPHIES

Barr, Mary-Margaret H., *A Century of Voltaire Study: a bibliography of writings on Voltaire, 1825–1925* (New York: Institute of French Studies, 1929), 123 pp.
———, "Bibliographical data on Voltaire from 1926 to 1930," *Modern Language Notes* (1933), 48: 292–307.
———, "Bibliographical data on Voltaire from 1931 to 1940," *Modern Language Notes* (1941), 56: 563–82.
Bengesco, Georges, *Voltaire: Bibliographie de ses oeuvres.* (Rouveyre et Blond: Vol. I; Perrin Vol. 2–4; 1882–1890). 4 vols.
   Barr, Bengesco, and Cabeen should prove adequate bibliographical instruments for most Voltairean research. Helpful assistance in using Bengesco can be found in Jean Malcolm's *Table de la Bibliographie de Voltaire par Bengesco* (Geneva: Institut et Musée Voltaire, 1953); Francis J. Crowley's "Addition to Bengesco's Bibliographies" (*Modern Language Notes*, 1952); and Theodore Besterman's *Quelques éditions anciennes de Voltaire inconnues à Bengesco* (Geneva: Institut et Musée Voltaire, 1954).
Cabeen, D. C. (General Editor): *A Critical Bibliography of French Literature* (New York: Syracuse Univ. Press, 1951); George R. Havens and Donald F. Bond, eds., Vol. IV, pp. 182–207 (Voltaire section). A *Supplement* to Vol. IV (eighteenth century, Richard A. Brooks, ed.) should be out in 1966 that will bring the critical bibliography of the eighteenth century up to date.

PRINCIPAL COLLECTED EDITIONS

Oeuvres de Voltaire: Beuchot, ed. (Paris: Lefèvre, 1828–1840, 72 vols.).

Oeuvres de Voltaire: Louis Moland, ed. (Paris: Garnier, 1877–1885, 52 vols.).
> The Moland edition is the last edition of Voltaire's completed works and the one invariably referred to by scholars. The principal difference is the addition of the volumes of correspondence, which now have been superseded by the scholarly and definitive edition of *Voltaire's Correspondence* by Theodore Besterman that has more than doubled the number of letters contained in the Moland edition.

Voltaire's Correspondence: Theodore Besterman, ed. (Institut et Musée Voltaire, Geneva, 1953–1966, 102 vols. of text, 5 vols. of index).
> This scholarly and definitive edition contains more than 20,000 letters and supersedes the volumes of correspondence of the Moland edition.

CRITICAL EDITIONS OF
INDIVIDUAL WORKS

Lanson, Gustave, *Les Lettres philosophiques* (Paris: Hachette, 1909), 1st ed. in *Grands écrivains français* series, Paris, 1906.

Morize, André, *L'Apologie du luxe au 18e siècle et le Mondain de Voltaire, étude critique sur le Mondain et ses sources* (Paris: Didier, 1909).

Morize, André, *Candide ou l'optimisme* (Paris: Hachette, 1913).

Ascoli, Georges, *Zadig ou la Destinée, édition critique* (Paris: Hachette, 1929, 2 vols.).

Jones, William R., *L'Ingénu* (Paris: Minard, 1957—original publication, 1936).

Patterson, H. Temple (Mrs.), *Traité de métaphysique* (Manchester: Manchester Univ. Press, 1937).

Crowley, Francis J., *Poème sur la Loi Naturelle* (Berkeley: Calif. Univ. Press, 1938).

Carcassonne, E., *Le Temple du goût* (Geneva: Droz, 1938).

Olivier, J. J., *Sémiramis* (Paris: Droz, 1946).

Wade, Ira O., *Voltaire's Micromégas; A Study in the Fusion of Science, Myth and Art* (Princeton: Princeton Univ. Press, 1950).

Pomeau, René, *Le Taureau blanc* (Paris: Nizet, 1957).

GENERAL BACKGROUND WORKS

Becker, Carl, *The Heavenly City of Eighteenth-Century Philosophers* (New York: Yale Univ. Press, 1932).

Cassirer, Ernst, *Die Philosophie der Aufklärung* (Tübingen: Mohr, 1932). English tr. by F. C. A. Koelln and J. P. Pettegrove, *The Philosophy of the Enlightenment* (Princeton: Princeton Univ. Press, 1951).
   Written by a sound philosophical mind, it represents a profound study of the Enlightenment.

Crocker, Lester G., *An Age of Crisis: Man and World in Eighteenth-Century French Thought* (Baltimore: Johns Hopkins Press, 1959).

———, *Nature and Culture: Ethical Thought in the French Enlightenment* (Baltimore: Johns Hopkins Press, 1963).
   Both books are stimulating works written in a philosophical vein; they probe deeply and wisely into the broad reaches of eighteenth-century thought, ethics, and philosophy.

Desnoiresterres, G., *Voltaire et la société de son temps* (2nd ed. Paris: Didier, 1867–1876, 8 vols.).
   For over half a century this monumental work has set the tone and direction of Voltaire criticism. Still quite useful for general background.

Folkierski, Wladyslaw, *Entre le classicisme et le romantisme* (Paris: Champion, 1925).

Havens, George R., *The Age of Ideas* (New York, 1955).
   A good general background of the age for non-specialist and specialist alike.

Hazard, Paul, *La Crise de la conscience européenne, 1680–1715* (Paris: Boivin, 1935, 3 vols.).

———, *La Pensée européenne au XVIIIe Siècle; de Montesquieu à Lessing* (Paris: Boivin, 1946, 3 vols.).

Martin, Kingsley, *French Liberal Thought in the Eighteenth Century* (Boston: Little, Brown, 1929).

Mornet, Daniel, *La Pensée française au XVIIIe siècle* (Paris: Colin, 2nd ed. 1929).

————, *Les Origines intellectuelles de la Révolution française, 1715–1787* (Paris: Colin, 1933).
Les Origines of Mornet complements nicely the equally excellent work of Hazard, *La Crise*.

Sée, Henri, *L'Evolution de la pensée politique en France au XVIIIe siècle* (Paris: Giard, 1925).

SCHOLARLY AND CRITICAL WORKS

Besterman, Theodore, *Lettres d'amour de Voltaire à sa nièce* (Paris: Plon, 1957).
————, ed., *Studies on Voltaire and the eighteenth century* (Geneva: Institut et Musée Voltaire, 1955–1966. 44 vols. to date).
One of the richest mines of articles and monographs on the eighteenth century in general and Voltaire in particular.
————, *Voltaire's Notebooks* (Geneva: Institut et Musée Voltaire, 1952, 2 vols.).
The debt Voltaire scholars owe Theodore Besterman is incalculable. His contributions are too many to enumerate, but undoubtedly the greatest effort of his remarkable career is the successful conclusion of the monumental task started in 1953 of publishing a definitive and scholarly edition of Voltaire's correspondence. It is safe to say that no one in the world today has a more thorough knowledge of Voltaire than Mr. Besterman, who has literally lived and breathed Voltaire at Les Délices these many years.

Bottiglia, William F., *Voltaire's Candide: Analysis of a classic* (Geneva: Institut et Musée Voltaire, 1st ed. 1957; 2nd, 1964), *Studies on Voltaire*, VII and VIIA.
The most recent comprehensive study of *Candide*—detailed and scholarly, especially useful for specialists. The completely revised second edition is much more readable and useful.

Brailsford, Henry N., *Voltaire* (London: Butterworth, 1935).
This work and those listed for Dorothy McGhee and Ruth Flowers, plus Raymond Naves' *Le Goût de Voltaire* and Lanson's *L'Art de la prose* are the most useful general studies of Voltaire's style.

Brumfitt, J. H., *Voltaire, historian* (Oxford, 1958).

Probably the most helpful reference for the historical ideas of Voltaire.

Chaponnière, Paul, *Voltaire chez les Calvinistes* (Paris: Perrin, 1936).
An excellent and measured treatment of the subject.

Conlon, P. M., *Voltaire's Literary Career from 1728 to 1750* (Geneva: Institut et Musée Voltaire, 1960), *Studies on Voltaire*, XIV.

Diaz, Furio, *Voltaire, storico* (Torino: Einaudi, 1959).

Endore, Guy, *The Heart and the Mind: The Story of Rousseau and Voltaire* (London: W. H. Allen, 1962).

Fitch, Robert E., *Voltaire's philosophic procedure. A Case-Study in the history of ideas* (Oregon: The News-Times Pub. Co., 1935).

Flowers, Ruth C., *Voltaire's stylistic transformation of Rabelaisian satirical devices* (Washington: Catholic Univ. of Amer. Press, 1951).

Gay, Peter, *Voltaire's politics* (Princeton: Princeton Univ. Press, 1959).

Havens, G. R., and N. L. Torrey, *Voltaire's Catalogue of his library at Ferney* (Geneva, 1959); *Studies on Voltaire* IX, 9–258.

Kozminski, Léon, *Voltaire financier* (Paris: Presses Universitaires, 1929), 338 pp.

Lancaster, Henry Carrington, *French tragedy in the time of Louis XV and Voltaire, 1715–1774* (Baltimore: Johns Hopkins Press, 1950, 2 vols.).

Lanson, Gustave, *L'Art de la prose* (Paris: Librairie des Annales, 1909).

———, *Voltaire* (Paris: Hachette, 1960; 1st ed., 1906). English tr. by Robert A. Wagoner, *Voltaire* (New York: John Wiley, 1966).
After more than a half century, this classic study is still probably the best single work on Voltaire.

Lion, Henri, *Les Tragédies et les théories dramatiques de Voltaire* (Paris, 1895).
This detailed and comprehensive analysis of Voltaire's role in the theater can be very useful to anyone working in this field.

Lounsbury, Thomas R., *Shakespeare and Voltaire* (London, 1902).
Despite its publication date, still an interesting and informative treatment.

Lowenstein, Robert, *Voltaire as an historian of seventeenth-*

century French drama (Baltimore: Johns Hopkins Press, 1935).

Maestro, Marcello T., *Voltaire and Beccaria as Reformers of Criminal Law* (New York: Columbia Univ. Press, 1942).

May, Georges, *Le Dilemme du Roman au XVIIIe siècle* (Paris: Presses Universitaires de la France, 1963).

McGhee, Dorothy, *Voltaire's Narrative Devices as considered in the author's contes philosophiques* (Menasha, 1933).

Morley, John, *Voltaire* (London, 1872; Macmillan, 1913). This study and Norman L. Torrey's *Spirit of Voltaire* are considered the best works on Voltaire in English. Morley is readable, interesting and scholarly.

Naves, Raymond, *Le Goût de Voltaire* (Paris: Garnier, 1938).
———, *Voltaire, l'homme et l'oeuvre* (Paris: Boivin, 1942). These and all of Raymond Naves' works on Voltaire are sound and important contributions. His premature death was a tremendous loss to Voltairean scholarship.

Pomeau, René, *Voltaire par lui-même* (Paris: Seuil, 1955).
———, *La Religion de Voltaire* (Paris: Nizet, 1956). *La Religion* is a thorough and scholarly work by one of France's most prolific and profound Voltairean scholars.

Robertson, J. M., *Voltaire* (London: Watts, 1922).

Rowe, Constance, *Voltaire and the State* (New York: Columbia Univ. Press, 1955).

Torrey, Norman L., *Voltaire and The English Deists* (New Haven: Yale Univ. Press, 1930).
———, *The Spirit of Voltaire* (New York: Columbia Univ. Press, 1938). For a sympathetic understanding of the ideas and "spirit" of Voltaire, nothing surpasses this delightfully written book. It offers a felicitous combination of original thought and research.

Wade, Ira O., *Voltaire and Mme du Châtelet; an essay on the intellectual activity at Cirey* (Princeton: Princeton Univ. Press, 1941), 241 pp.
———, *Studies on Voltaire* (Princeton: Princeton Univ. Press, 1947).
———, *The Search for a new Voltaire* (Transactions of the American Philosophical Society, Philadelphia), XLVIII (July 1958).

Waldinger, Renée, *Voltaire and Reform in the light of the French Revolution* (Paris: Minard, 1959).

CHRONOLOGY

No attempt will be made to be all-inclusive. Instead, only the important events and literary milestones of a very complex and productive life will be indicated, following the example of René Pomeau, whose excellent chronologies in *Voltaire par lui-même* and his edition of *Voltaire: Oeuvres historiques* (Pléiade) have served as guides.

1694: November 21, birth of François-Marie Arouet in Paris.
1704: Enters Louis-le-Grand, *lycée* run by Jesuits; remains for seven years, after which he makes first attempt to study law.
1713: Goes to La Haye as secretary of Châteauneuf, Ambassador. Pimpette affair causes dismissal and incurs displeasure of father.
1715: Already working on *Oedipe* and *La Henriade* when Louis XIV dies. Second attempt at law also a failure; influence of "Society of the Temple."
1716: Experiences first taste of royal displeasure; "exiled" to Sully-sur-Loire for two works written against Regent.
1717: Imprisoned in Bastille May 16 for period of 11 months.
1718: *Oedipe* enthusiastically acclaimed by unrestrained society of Regency; compared with Corneille and Racine; changes name to de Voltaire. For a few years leads life of dilettantism and libertinism during which he frequents best salons of day.
1722: Death of father. "Epître à Uranie"; clash with J. B. Rousseau reaches climax over latter's "Ode à la Postérité."
1723: Contracts smallpox; friendship of famous actress Adrienne Lecouvreur, then mistress of d'Argental. First publication of *La Henriade* as *La Ligue*.
1725: Beaten by lackeys of Chevalier de Rohan at time when everything had combined to convince him of his unconditional acceptance in highest society.

1726: Again victim of *lettre de cachet;* imprisoned in Bastille but shortly exiled to England, where he makes contact with English men of letters and men in government; even presented to King George I in 1727.

1729: Return to France followed by intense literary activity.

1730: Death of Mlle Lecouvreur. Denial by church of decent burial elicits "Ode sur la Mort de Mlle Lecouvreur." *Brutus.*

1731: *Histoire de Charles XII.*

1732: Love theme insured triumph of *Zaïre,* first real success since *Oedipe.*

1733: Start of liaison with Emilie du Châtelet. *Temple du Goût* creates much antagonism from traditionalists who could not bear to see their cherished literary figures criticized.

1734: *Lettres philosophiques* after English publication in London in 1733. Scandal ensues, seeks refuge at Cirey with Emilie. *Adelaïde du Guesclin* and "Traité de la métaphysique."

1735: *La Mort de César.* Long visit at Cirey by Italian savant Algarotti. Voltaire working on several works, notably "Discours en vers sur l'homme" (7 Discours, 1734–1737) and throughout the thirties and forties on *La Pucelle.*

1736: Future Frederick II starts corresponding with Voltaire. *Alzire* and "Le Mondain."

1737: "Les Eléments de la philosophie de Newton"; arrest of Armand, brother of Voltaire, for Jansenist activities.

1738: Newly married niece, Mme. Denis (former Marie-Louis Mignot) visits Cirey. Former disciple Desfontaines publishes satire, *Voltairomanie.* Emilie and Voltaire compete for prize with theses on the nature of fire.

1739: First chapters of *Siècle de Louis XIV* seized by police, he embarks on larger project, *Histoire générale,* of which *Siècle* later forms last segment.

1740: Frederick II ascends throne and shortly after invades Silesia. First meeting between Frederick and Voltaire at Moyland.

1741: War of Succession (Austria). Voltaire attempts diplomacy, but too ingenuous for wily Frederick and places too much reliance upon reason. Success of *Mahomet* in Lille.

1742: Three representations of *Mahomet* in Paris, then withdrawn because of cabals. Official diplomatic mission to get Frederick to become ally of France is not successful.

1743: Death of Cardinal de Fleury. More diplomatic ventures. Frederick tries to keep Voltaire in Prussia. *Mérope,* his purest tragedy.

1744: Voltaire's favor at court grows, thanks to friendship of D'Argenson, friend of school days, who becomes Minister of Foreign Affairs; also due to friendship of Dukes de Richelieu and de La Vallière and the king's mistresses: Mme. de Châteauroux, Mme. d'Etioles, and Mme. de Pompadour.

1745: Death of brother, Armand Arouet. Voltaire named Historiographer Royal (writes "Poème de Fontenoy"); dedicates *Mahomet* to Pope; and in *Mercure de France* publishes "Nouveau plan d'une histoire de l'esprit humain," later first part of *Essai sur les moeurs.*

1746: Elected to French Academy; made Gentilhomme Ordinaire de la Chambre du Roi. With newly acquired prestige tends to crush enemies but protects young men of talent like Marmontel, d'Alembert, and Vauvenargues. *Le Monde comme il va, vision de Babouc.*

1747: Flight to Sceaux (Duchesse du Maine) after *jeu de la reine* incident. *Zadig.*

1748: Voltaire finds Emilie in arms of new lover Saint-Lambert. *Sémiramis.*

1749: Death of Emilie in childbirth; Voltaire distraught at loss.

1750: Leaves France for Berlin, and for first few months Voltaire, the Chamberlain of the King, leads a life of enchantment, despite irritating chore of correcting Frederick's poetry. Start of Hirschell affair causes relationship with Frederick to worsen.

1751: Secretary Longchamp steals manuscript of histories— Voltaire often plagued by theft of manuscripts. Publication of *Siècle de Louis XIV.*

1752: *Histoire de la guerre de 1741.* Voltaire publicly defends Koenig against Maupertuis, President of Berlin Academy, thereby angering Frederick further. La Beaumelle, friend of Maupertuis, publishes distorted edition of *Siècle.* Voltaire publishes "Diatribe du docteur Akakia"—final indignity in eyes of disenchanted Frederick. "Poème sur la Loi Naturelle" and *Micromégas.*

1753: *Supplément au Siècle* to combat La Beaumelle's edition. Leaves Berlin; unhappy incident at Frankfort. *Annales de l'Empire.*

1754:   Reaches Geneva, after working for weeks in monastery.

1755:   Earthquake in Lisbon. Quickly writes "Poème sur le désastre de Lisbonne," published early part of 1756 along with "Poème sur la Loi Naturelle." (J.-J. Rousseau answered with "Lettre sur la Providence," Aug. 1756). Buys Les Délices in Geneva. *Orphelin de la Chine.*

1756:   *Essai sur les moeurs.* Start of Seven Years' War. D'Alembert at Les Délices works on article "Génève" for *Encyclopédie* (1757). Degree of Voltaire's collaboration undetermined. This article defending theater draws impassioned but somewhat irrational response from Rousseau in his famous *Lettre à d'Alembert sur les spectacles,* 1758.

1757:   Acts as intermediary between France and Frederick II, who is momentarily suffering military reverses.

1758:   Buys Ferney in October and in December, Tournay. Defection of d'Alembert.

1759:   "Histoire d'un bon Bramin"; *Candide ou l'Optimisme; Histoire de l'Empire de Russie sous Pierre le Grand,* requested by Russian Ambassador in 1757.

1760:   *Tancrède.* J.-J. Rousseau breaks with Voltaire—break becomes irrevocable in 1764 after Rousseau's publication of *Lettres écrites de la montagne,* in which he has designated Voltaire as author of inflammable *Sermon des cinquante,* written around 1752 but not published until 1762. Voltaire counterattacks without mercy or restraint in *Sentiment des citoyens,* Dec. 1764.

1761:   Begins *Commentaire sur Corneille* to help Marie Corneille, great-grandniece of playwright, with dowry. Close reading of all of Corneille causes Voltaire's opinion of Corneille to drop, and this creates more enemies for Voltaire. Writes four "Lettres à M de Voltaire sur la *Nouvelle Héloise,*" supposedly written by the marquis de Ximénès.

1762:   Intensifies campaign to save pastor Rochette sentenced to die in Toulouse; disseminates "Extrait du Testament de Meslier" and *Sermon des cinquante.* Execution of Jean Calas March 10 in Toulouse for supposedly having hanged his son to prevent his conversion to Catholicism. Voltaire undertakes formidable task of rehabilitation.

1763:   *Siècle de Louis XV;* "Traité sur la tolérance"; marriage of Marie Corneille. Review of Calas trial ordered.

1764: *Commentaire sur Corneille;* first edition of *Dictionnaire philosophique* as *Dictionnaire portatif;* "Discours aux Welches," Voltaire's pejorative name for provincial-minded and bigoted French. *Sentiment des citoyens* attacks Rousseau. The Sirvens, after having fled to safety in Lausanne, are condemned to death for supposedly having drowned their daughter. Seek Voltaire's assistance, which he gives unreservedly after Calas rehabilitation.

1765: *Dictionnaire philosophique.* Vindication of Calas. "Philosophie de l'histoire" becomes Introduction of *Essai sur les moeurs.* Arrest of Chevalier de La Barre; D'Etallonde had already fled to Prussia with the aid of Voltaire.

1766: *Le Philosophe ignorant;* "Commentaire sur le livre des délits et des peines." In July the Chevalier de La Barre is decapitated and burned, along with copy of *Dictionnaire philosophique.* Execution of Comte de Lally; Voltaire takes up his defense, and clamors for all-out *philosophe* counterattack. Incensed by others' indifference.

1767: *L'Ingénu;* "Les Questions de Zapata"; "L'Examen important de Milord Bolingbroke"; enlarges new edition of *Siècle de Louis XIV.*

1768: "L'Homme aux quarante écus." Grants refuge at Ferney and at newly formed colony of Versoix to skilled artisans who are fleeing Geneva because of underprivileged status. Voltaire at first supports his aristocratic friends, but later defends the *natifs.*

1769: Return of Mme. Denis to Ferney 18 months after Voltaire had bundled her off to Paris for complicity with La Harpe in theft of manuscripts in 1768. Works on Martin case—a farmer executed on the wheel for a crime to which someone else later confessed.

1770: Starts work on 9 vols. of *Questions sur l'Encyclopédie,* completed in 1772. Many skilled watchmakers from among *natifs* establish themselves at Ferney, aided by their leader Auzière. Writes vigorous refutation of d'Holbach's materialism and atheism in *Système de la nature* (1770). Mme. Necker takes initiative in subscription for Pigalle sculpture of Voltaire.

1771: Sirvens cleared by Parliament of Toulouse after seven years' fight, during which Voltaire had engaged Elie de Beaumont, defender of Calas, to fight the case and had also got up subscription to which Frederick II, Catherine the Great, and Stanislas A. Poniatowski, King of Poland, had contributed generously.

1773: "Fragment sur le procès criminel de Montbailli," in defense of Montbailli who had been killed on the wheel in 1770. Voltaire had him declared innocent.

1774: Death of Louis XV, May 10. Voltaire welcomes enthusiastically Turgot's successive appointments as Minister of Finance, Controller-General, and Secretary of State.

1775: D'Etallonde staying at Ferney. Writes "Le Cri du sang innocent" in behalf of La Barre, but never succeeds in clearing his name. During the last years many persons, too numerous to list, stay at Ferney for varying periods of time.

1776: "Prix de la justice et de l'humanité."

1777: Voltaire hurt by snub paid him by Joseph II, young Emperor of Austria, who fails to stop for visit when traveling through Ferney.

1778: Return to Paris after absence of twenty-eight years. Apotheosis at theater where his *Irène* is being performed. Last days brightened by news that Lally has been rehabilitated. Dies May 30, 1778.

INDEX